PEARSON　　　ALWAYS LEARNING

Michael Abrams • Dr. Michael L. Faulkner
Andrea Nierenberg

Networking for Veterans

A Guidebook for a Successful Military Transition into the Civilian Workforce

Pearson Learning Solutions, 501 Boylston Street, Suite 900, Boston, MA 02116
A Pearson Education Company
www.pearsoned.com

Printed in the United States of America

1 2 3 4 5 6 7 8 9 10 V011 17 16 15 14 13 12

000200010271308888

JH/CM

ISBN 10: 1-256-88887-7
ISBN 13: 978-1-256-88887-1

DEDICATION

This book is dedicated to the 6,586 service members who
have been killed fighting in Iraq and Afghanistan. We owe it to each
one of these men and women to ensure we make a successful transition
back home and live productive and fulfilling lives.

ACKNOWLEDGMENTS

This is the hardest page for us to write. There are so many people who we want to thank personally and give credit for making us better networkers, and more importantly, better people. For Andrea, this book has been a work in progress for nearly 20 years. For Dr. Mike Faulkner, it's been 40 years in the making since struggling and successfully overcoming the challenges of his military transition during the Vietnam War.

We would first like to thank our editor, Frank Burrows, and everyone at Pearson Learning Solutions for all their guidance, hard work, and dedication in bringing this book to life.

Andrea would like to give a special thanks to Trudy and the late Bill Mitchell. Bill was a World War II veteran who earned the Purple Heart and Bronze Star for his actions. He went on to become an oil entrepreneur and philanthropist to Deaconess Hospital and the University of Southern Indiana, in addition to many other charities and organizations. Trudy and Bill have also been large supporters of the Wounded Warriors. They are two of the most special people who have been on this earth and Trudy continues to carry on with the work of her wonderful husband after 68 years of wedded bliss.

Mike would like to thank his family, who supported him unconditionally through seven years on active duty as well as during his military transition. You were always there.

Mike would also like to thank a few veterans and civilian professionals in the NYC community who helped him with his military transition, and as a result, indirectly assisted with the writing of this book: Gerry Byrne, Mark and Matt McMahon, Bill Murray, Kevin Gallagher, Chris Vasiliou, Rick Miners, Rich Sweeney, Peter Galasinao, Joe Lisi, Andrew Roberts, John and Lauren Carnes, Chris Wilkens, Brian Dorfler, Val Nicholas, Mike Scotti, Lucas Detor, and Stephen Clark.

Thanks to all for your help, support, and friendship.

Mike Abrams joined the Marine Corps following the September 11th attacks, serving on active duty for seven years and deploying to eastern Afghanistan with an infantry company as the artillery forward observer. After leaving active duty, Mike attended New York University's Stern School of Business, graduating with an M.B.A. in Finance and Entrepreneurship & Innovation. While in business school, Mike co-founded a veteran mentoring program called Four Block. The program focuses on providing professional development to student veterans and connecting them with internship opportunities and entry-level positions at corporations. Mike is currently a Producer at CNBC.

Dr. Michael L. Faulkner is a U.S. Marine Corps Vietnam veteran who served from 1964–1970 and rose to the rank of Staff Sergeant. He spent 30 years in a variety of leadership and management ("coaching") positions with Dun & Bradstreet, the Direct Marketing Association (DMA), and entrepreneurial start-ups, as well as helping run the family business before moving into the academic world. Today Michael is a professor at the Keller Graduate School of Management at DeVry University.

Michael is a member of MENSA, a former two-time national champion of Athletic Dueling, and an International Rotary Fellowship award winner. He has been published in peer review journals, dozens of magazines, newsletters, websites, and blogs, and has written half a dozen white papers, including one that was circulated to all elected members of Congress and the major media outlets. He has written or co-authored nine books and two one-act plays, which were both performed in regional theaters.

Andrea R. Nierenberg, best-selling author, speaker, and world-renowned business authority, is the force behind The Nierenberg Consulting Group.

Called a "networking success story" by *The Wall Street Journal,* Andrea founded The Nierenberg Consulting Group in 1993.

With a stellar 29 years as a leader in sales and marketing, Andrea is an in-demand business expert both at home and abroad. Her company partners with an array of the world's leading financial and media industry businesses.

In 2009, I retired from the United States Marine Corps after 20 years of active duty service. My own transition from the military was full of good fortune. I was lucky to have a mentor like former National Security Advisor General Jim Jones, who took a very special interest in my search for a second career. I was lucky to have a network of close friends who had successfully made their own transitions from the military to the private sector. And I was lucky to be hired by an organization like the U.S. Chamber of Commerce with President and CEO Tom Donohue, who understands and appreciates the value of hiring a veteran.

Many younger veterans are not that fortunate. Last year, the jobless rate for post-9/11 veterans was 50% higher than the national average at 12.1%, and veterans under the age of 25 faced a staggering 29.1% unemployment rate. These data are even more concerning given the additional one million service members who will be leaving active duty over the next five years.

In light of these challenges, the U.S. Chamber of Commerce and National Chamber Foundation launched *Hiring our Heroes*, a nationwide campaign to help veterans and military spouses find meaningful employment after serving our nation. With an aggressive goal of hosting 500 hiring fairs in its first two years, *Hiring Our Heroes* is the largest scale effort of its kind and was founded on the premise that transitioning military families often pursue career opportunities based on where they want to establish roots, versus what their best job prospects might be.

In close collaboration with a host of government, non-profit, and veteran service organizations, the strength of *Hiring Our Heroes* has been our ability to forge strong public–private partnerships and positively influence the employment of veterans and military spouses in hundreds of communities across America. Working with the Employer Support of the Guard and Reserve, the American Legion, the Department of Labor Veterans' Employment and Training Service, and the U.S. Department of Veterans Affairs, our grassroots efforts have helped 10,000 veterans and military spouses find jobs at more than 200 hiring fairs over a 15-month period starting in March of 2011.

Beyond our efforts to create a movement to address veteran unemployment at the local level, we must also tackle the systemic issues facing our nation's veterans before they leave the military and search for a second career. We must do a better job of helping transitioning service members prepare for the civilian workforce and make informed decisions about employment in the private sector.

For starters, we need to show them where the jobs are, what industries and sectors are hiring, and how to use their educational benefits to gain specific qualifications, so they can land one of the two million well paying jobs that President Obama mentioned in his 2012 State of the Union address. It is unconscionable that our newest generation of veterans is struggling to find work when millions of jobs go unfilled because we lack a trained workforce.

With that in mind, *Hiring Our Heroes* and the Institute for Veterans and Military Families at Syracuse University launched a program called *Fast Track*. Designed to show the critical paths to meaningful careers in growth sectors such as energy, health care, information technology (IT; including cyber security), transportation, and infrastructure, *Fast Track* helps veterans and transitioning service members make informed decisions about the use of the GI Bill to gain targeted employment opportunities. The program maps the 100 metropolitan areas with the fastest-growing job markets, and is populated with the educational and credentialing pathways to well paying, highly skilled careers.

To be clear, *Hiring Our Heroes* is not about charity. Companies that hire veterans gain a competitive advantage, and our nation should view the imminent drawdown of our armed forces as an opportunity. After World War II, millions of veterans reentered the workforce, and the massive infusion of talent helped the manufacturing sector to grow and America's economy, as a whole, to thrive. As we come out of this recession, transitioning post-9/11 veterans can help growing industries expand further and our economy prosper.

Veterans must also do their part to better market and brand their unique skill sets so they stand out in a tough job market. There are no handouts, and veterans must compete just like they did in uniform—on the rifle range, in the classroom, and in the field. Even with advanced technical skills, leadership experience, unparalleled discipline, and the ability to work well in teams, veterans cannot expect employers—and human resources managers, in particular—to understand their military background without a clear and concise explanation.

Personal branding is one of the biggest obstacles facing newer veterans. Few transitioning service members have developed a strong "elevator pitch," and I have personally witnessed many fail when they stepped in front of employers for the first time at dozens of *Hiring Our Heroes* fairs. Building a personal brand is not just about translating military occupational skills (MOS). Many pundits throw this idea around as the "big fix," but it's more than that. When veterans have less than 90 seconds to convince a company to hire them over someone who went straight into college after high school, a strong brand is critical. By focusing on intangible traits and using plain language to describe personal awards, deployments, schools, and leadership billets, veterans can demonstrate why they stand head and shoulders above their peers.

After seeing hundreds of younger veterans struggle through interviews at its hiring fairs, *Hiring Our Heroes* joined forces with Toyota and Medal of Honor recipient Dakota Meyer to create a personal branding guide that is being distributed to tens of thousands of veterans nationwide. In addition to being shared at *Hiring Our Heroes* events, the guide is also available online as part of a personal branding tool-kit that contains unique advice for members of the Marines, Army, Navy, and Air Force. Working alongside a company like Toyota that understands brand development and one of our nation's most recognizable younger veterans, *Hiring Our Heroes'* aim is to help transitioning service members tell a compelling story about their military service to potential employers and turn their next interview into a job.

Even with the necessary tools to build a personal brand and make an informed decision about employment, veterans must also develop a strong network once they leave the military if they want to land their dream job. Networking is the connective tissue for any successful career search. Without mentors and a network of friends and associates in the private sector, veterans will enter the civilian workforce blindly and oftentimes will run into a series of dead ends.

Given today's widespread use of social media, there is no shortage of opportunities to build an effective network. Google, Facebook, and LinkedIn can be launch-pads to connect with business professionals from specific industries who have prior military experience and have made difficult transitions themselves. In addition to providing networking opportunities at hundreds of hiring fairs across America, *Hiring Our Heroes* looks to these technologies and others as the glue for *Fast Track* and the Personal Branding initiative.

Networking for Veterans serves as an effective guide to help veterans make strong first impressions, build those initial connections into professional relationships, and finally turn interviews into job offers. This book is a great tool to prepare for and take advantage of programs like *Hiring Our Heroes* and hundreds of others around the country that are making a concerted effort to connect veterans with meaningful employment.

—Kevin Schmiegel, Executive Director, *Hiring Our Heroes*

HOW TO USE THIS BOOK

When I transitioned off active duty, I was completely unprepared. I had no idea what I wanted to do, had no understanding of the opportunities that were available to me, and thought I was entitled to a job. Seriously, I'm a combat Marine—not only am I endlessly more qualified than any nasty civilian out there, but I also served my country during a time of war. I should be able to land a job wherever I want, right?

I couldn't have been more wrong.

I really thought that employers would jump at the opportunity to hire a service member. But they didn't. I applied unsuccessfully to dozens upon dozens of online job postings. I was spraying my resume everywhere and praying to get a response. I received nothing back except automatically generated rejection emails. I was confused, frustrated, and I even began to think that getting off active duty was a big mistake.

I was absolutely ashamed to ask people for help, so I continued to try and figure things out on my own. I bought a couple of military transition books, visited every military recruitment website that I could find, and even tried working with a few headhunters. The more I looked for easy answers, the more frustrated I became with my transition.

Looking back, my big mistake was to believe that I could make a successful transition on my own.

If it wasn't for the support of my family and the many veterans in my community who took me under their wings, I don't know where I'd be right now. They taught me that the only way to figure things out was to get out there and talk to people. They showed me that there was a huge network of former military veterans and civilian professionals who were willing to sit down and assist me in making the right career decision. I just had to ask them. I learned that sitting down and speaking with a veteran or civilian professional about a career that I was interested in was much more helpful and informative than reading a book or visiting any number of websites.

This book isn't going to provide you with any easy answers. There is no secret step-by-step guide that if followed exactly will lead you to a six-figure salary. Rather this book will teach you how to develop relationships with the people in your community who are the most willing and able to help you figure out the best next step in your life and career, and then help you get there.

Nothing of value in life is ever quick and easy. Transitioning back home and starting a new career isn't going to happen overnight. In fact, it took me two years after transitioning to settle into a job that I genuinely enjoyed. I firmly believe that effective networking, building and sustaining personal and professional relationships, is the key to making a successful military transition. I want to show you how networking has worked for me, my veteran buddies, and my civilian friends. I hope you will enjoy, use, and most of all, profit from these words.

—Michael Abrams

Courtesy of Joshua Wartchow

WHAT YOU NEED TO KNOW BEFORE TRANSITIONING

NO ONE IS GOING TO GIVE YOU A JOB!

In the corporate world, transitioning veterans are not that special. It doesn't matter how many combat tours you completed, how many medals you received, or whether you were in the infantry or aviation supply. Most employers look at us like we're all the same because they don't really know what service members do on a day-to-day basis.

Remember that less than 1% of the U.S. population has served, so their knowledge of the military is limited to Hollywood movies, cable news, and the exaggerated stories they hear third hand from neighbors or co-workers. Think about it—can you speak intelligently about what a defense lawyer does other than what you see on *Law and*

Order? It's the same thing with us, so don't think that you're going to throw your military resume downrange and have dozens of companies fighting to hire you.

The truth of the matter is that America isn't at war: The military is. And the military doesn't explain that to service members. We think that everyone back home knows exactly what we do and understands how our skills translate to the corporate world. But they don't. As a result, the corporate world views veterans as a commodity rather than as individuals with specific and varying skills and experiences.

When you finally land that first job, you probably won't be in charge of anyone. You won't be mentoring other colleagues, influencing operations, or frankly, have responsibility for much of anything except yourself. You'll most likely be the low man on the totem pole so you can learn and acquire the technical competencies of your new job. Don't get down on yourself if you end up being a 28-year-old intern or if perhaps your new boss is several years younger than you are with considerably less leadership experience. Be prepared for this and don't take it personally. You have to pay your dues and learn the trade, just like you did in the military.

In the military there is no skipping ranks. You have to earn each stripe with hard work and experience. Could you imagine if the Army took the honors grad at boot camp and made him your squad leader in Afghanistan? There's just no way that would happen. So why would a company do the same thing with you? It's okay if you have to take a few steps back in order to take a thousand steps forward. Rarely will a veteran land a civilian job that is equivalent to the responsibility, authority, and compensation that he or she had in the military.

This is why it's so important to search for a career and not just settle for a job. If you choose to pursue a job because it pays well or comes with an impressive title, chances are you won't find the work very fulfilling and may end up quitting after a few months. Then you'll be back to square one again. But if you network with people, do your research, ask questions, and make an informed decision about a career that you genuinely enjoy, regardless of the starting pay or job title, you'll be a happier, harder working person. And in no time, your salary and responsibility will catch up to the value you bring to the company. Don't let your ego dictate your destiny.

FOCUS ON TAKING THE "HIGH GROUND"

In 2006, in the midst of our nation's two longest wars, Generals David Petreaus and James Amos took the hard lessons we've learned to date in Iraq and Afghanistan and re-wrote the Army and Marine Corps' counterinsurgency manual. The revised manual outlined a new strategy for how to fight and win an insurgency in the 21st century.

But the new strategy centered on a familiar principle that transcends centuries of war: winning the high ground.

In previous wars, like World War II, the high ground, or the most advantageous place to be on the battlefield, was an elevated piece of terrain such as a hill or a mountain from which a unit could best defend themselves, build up their forces, and then advance to the next objective.

But the wars in Iraq and Afghanistan are anything but conventional conflicts. We can't battle Al Qaeda the same way we did the Germans—sitting on top of a hill with superior firepower is no longer an advantageous position. In fact it's actually counterproductive when fighting an insurgency or an enemy that blends in with the local population. Generals Petreaus and Amos argued that the "high ground" in this type of asymmetric conflict is really the indigenous people.

In order to win this "terrain" we have to come off the hill and immerse ourselves in the community. We need to create relationships with the local people, understand their fears and needs, provide security, and show them that working with us is more prosperous than siding with the insurgents. We have to win their hearts and minds. It's personal. It's face-to-face combat. The only way to win the war is to create one positive relationship at a time.

Your military transition resembles fighting an insurgency. You can't just sit at home behind a computer and fling email at people. Nor can you depend solely on the traditional "formal" tools of job hunting such as answering ads, posting resumes on electronic job boards, hiring personal career coaches, signing up with recruiters or placement firms, and going to cattle call–type job fairs. There is overwhelming evidence that demonstrates that "informal" tools like networking are far more effective in the job search. You have to get out there and build relationships with the people in your community, ask questions, discover new opportunities, learn about different careers, and figure out how you're going to continue to live a life of service and honor.

The "high ground" in your military transition is the people in your community. Win this terrain and you'll have the information and opportunities you need to figure out the best next step in your life and career.

FIND STRENGTH IN SERVING OTHERS

When the going gets tough, we have a saying in the Marine Corps: Don't go internal. When you're in an uncomfortable or painful situation, it's only natural to focus on the discomfort you're experiencing and begin to feel sorry for yourself, like when it's 0300, you've been up for 35 hours straight, you're soaking wet, and the mission is a total cluster. Instead of staying focused on the mission at hand, you begin to let your discomfort consume your thoughts and you say things to yourself like, "Man, when will this damn patrol be over so I can get out of these wet clothes and go to bed?"

When you begin to feel sorry for yourself, or "go internal," you allow yourself to become weak and you put others around you at risk because you're focusing on the discomfort you're feeling instead of what you're supposed to be thinking about.

Much like your time in service, your military transition isn't going to be a rose garden. In fact, at times, it's going to be pretty unpleasant. But the thing that got us through the hard times during our military service was our commitment to putting the welfare of others ahead of ourselves. Think about it: Whenever we go internal, whenever we start thinking about ourselves, we get weaker. But when we think about the mission and focus on serving and helping others, we get stronger—and when that happens, nothing can get in our way.

The military is perhaps the most diverse organization in the world. And it's the ability to harness this diversity and channel it toward a common goal that makes us the greatest fighting force on the planet. And there's one common denominator that every single service member shares: a desire to serve something greater than themselves. This is our strength. This is what separates us from most of the 99% that chose not to serve our country.

It's extremely easy to go internal when making your transition. Trying to figure out what career to pursue or what you want to do with your life is a daunting task. It's overwhelming and it's exacerbated by the fact that you no longer have your buddies around to kick you in the butt when you start to feel sorry for yourself.

When you start to get discouraged and frustrated during your transition, and you can begin to feel yourself going internal, draw strength and direction from your inherent desire to serve something greater than yourself. Ask yourself:

- How can I make a positive difference in the lives of others?
- What kind of service can I provide to my community?
- What can I do to make the people around me better?

Service is your guiding principle through your transition. When you joined the military, you raised your right hand and swore to serve the nation. When you left, no one told you to put your hand back down. You never stop serving; you're just choosing to serve in another capacity.

When the going gets tough, don't go internal. Focus your energy on becoming an asset to your community, and you will find your way.

CHOOSE TO BE SUCCESSFUL

When you decided to join the military, you chose to be successful. You chose to hold yourself to a higher standard and to take the road less traveled. Your military transition presents another opportunity for you to choose whether you will have maximum control over your own pathway to life's success or not.

Let's be clear about one thing—you have not been chosen by some cosmic alignment or identified in any way as someone extra special. While individually you are unique and special because you are a member of one of the world's most respected clubs—U.S. military veterans—everyone, including non-veterans, will have the same opportunity to take control of their success at some point in their lives. Unfortunately, and this is where you can begin to separate yourself, the vast majority of people will not recognize this moment of opportunity when it comes and therefore they will not get the same benefits that you will if you make the right choice. What separates you from them is that you are reading this book and opening your mind to the possibilities that await you.

The reason this missed opportunity is unfortunate for others is because this is one of the few egalitarian moments in life when individuals, such as you, will have the opportunity to experience near perfect equality of opportunity for your own future.

Psychologists call this belief in self-empowerment an "internal locus of control." Skeptics and doubters are those who prefer to live their lives among flocks of others like themselves, who tend to dress alike, look alike, talk alike, work alike, think alike, act alike, believe alike, and like as well as dislike alike.

These people want you to believe life has a kind of predestined pathway. These people believe life is a linear path in which certain things are expected of you at certain times and certain things either come your way or they don't. In other words, they want you to believe that you have no control over your life.

Many psychologists believe in the self-concept theory (SCT), which states that many of the successes and failures people experience in their careers and lives are closely tied to the way in which they view themselves through their relationships with other people, including of course their parents, teachers, fellow veterans (including officers and noncoms), spouses, partners, bosses, managers, and supervisors.

There are three critical points to the SCT. First, the self-concept is learned; we are not born with it. We learn it through repeated experiences and our expectations about the outcome of those experiences, particularly with persons in powerful or influential roles. Generally a person's military experiences are an affirmation of the SCT. It is natural for U.S. military personnel to feel that they are a cut above because of their unique experiences.

Second, it is organized by our minds. We organize and then use as necessary the appropriate feelings, beliefs, and worldview of self-empowerment because we generally desire order and harmony in our lives. Lastly, the SCT is dynamic, meaning that the individual views the world not in isolation, but rather in relation to one's self-concept, which is subject to continuous reevaluation as one attempts to assimilate new ideas and get rid of old ones. Individuals will attempt to maintain their self-concept regardless of how helpful or damaging to themselves or others it becomes. Some individuals who will often sacrifice physical and financial comfort, and even their own safety, for emotional satisfaction to avoid change, display this truth.

Individuals experience anxiety because of a loss of self-esteem, and anything that negatively impacts self-concept risks depleting self-esteem. U.S. military veterans can make the SCT work for them or allow it to work against them. Most importantly, it is within each individual's control. Some people accept this while other people reject it. If you accept it, you exercise an internal locus of control and are ready to make the right choices to control your own life.

There are some people who believe life is full of unexpected randomness and troubles that will continually "pop-up," negating any preparations or plans we make. These people believe that the best we can do is manage these problems and obstacles and live with whatever the outcome may be.

We have examined and experienced the solutions for dealing with a wide range of issues that we are sure you have thought about or have been struggling with in your life: how to adjust to civilian life; which of your military experiences and skills will be helpful to you in looking for a job and building a career; how to overcome obstacles and problems with living and working in the civilian community; dealing with your fears, loneliness, and career aspirations; trying to cope with concerns about job search issues; worrying about how to meet people; managing your fear of public speaking; how to make new friends; and many, many other life issues that were not part of or were not prominent in your military life.

Most of these issues and problems you are thinking about don't have to be faced alone. In fact, you should not face them alone. If Chesty Puller had a Sergeant Major to help him get through the day, what makes any one of us think we can handle life by ourselves? Do not be afraid or egotistical or too wrapped in trying to prove you can be tough and resourceful to think you don't need the help of other people. You do. Only a fool believes that he or she can succeed alone.

Personal networking is, without a doubt, the most effective technique and tool used by the most successful individuals in all walks of life, regardless of gender, religion, industry, or profession, and at every age, in every social situation, and in all geographic areas.

Your invitation to self-fulfilling empowerment will be automatic once you learn about the power of personal networking and then decide to embrace the techniques of it. This isn't the tool of a secret society. Just about everybody has the opportunity to choose to learn the techniques and take up the tools of networking for success. However, experience and history have shown that only few will take the path.

Courtesy of Shutterstock.com

UNDERSTAND WHY NETWORKING IS SO IMPORTANT TO MAKING A SUCCESSFUL MILITARY TRANSITION

Was there ever a time when you went on a combat patrol by yourself? Of course there wasn't. Any time you left the wire, you were with your squad—or in other words, you were with a network of soldiers who looked after one another. Why? Because you were stronger together than you were individually. It's common sense, right? In order to be successful back here at home, you also need a squad of people that will have your back. The only difference is, back here at home you have to create your own squad. No one is assigned to

9

have your back anymore. In this chapter we discuss the foundational elements of how you can begin to create a professional network that will support you in making the right decisions for a successful transition back home.

There is a great deal of research and empirical evidence that proves something you probably know intuitively: Networking works for those who choose to network. It is, by an enormous margin, the single most effective technique for effective and productive job hunting (even during an economic downturn).

In 2008, the U.S. Department of Labor reported that more than 70% of all newly created jobs in the last decade were never posted or announced anywhere. Furthermore, more than 60% of replacement jobs were handled in the same manner. These jobs were not posted on any website, advertised on a classified page, or listed with any headhunter or recruiter. These jobs were filled by professional acquaintances in the hiring manager's network.

We have seen this issue discussed in other research, in other studies, and by other authors as well. Depending on the study or book one is quoting, the percentage of jobs filled by networking varies from 60% to 85%. The exact number is not the issue. The important issue is simply that the overwhelming number of jobs in America is filled through the process of networking. If you do not use networking skills, then you surrender many job, life, and other opportunities to people who do embrace networking. As a post–9/11 veteran, you deserve to gain the benefits of networking, but you have to reach out and take them. No one is going to network for you.

Some economists believe that unemployment will be a societal problem in America for years to come. Networking could be the difference between being part of the pool of military veterans working in low-level, unsatisfying jobs and those who move their careers along regardless of the state of economy.

Not only is the process of networking the way most people are hired by employers, in addition interpersonal traits (networking skills) are among the top characteristics sought after by employers. In a number of research studies conducted over the past ten years, senior managers at a wide range of businesses were asked about what they were looking for in recent college graduates.

The following is what these managers said they value most in terms of skills, traits, characteristics, and talents:

- Good communication skills
- Interpersonal skills
- Ability to find and fix problems

- Enthusiasm
- High energy level
- Strength of character
- Self-confidence
- Motivation
- Leadership skills
- Quick adaptability to change and uncertainty
- Commitment to lifetime learning
- Commitment to excellence
- Being a team player
- Willingness to take some risks
- Willingness to face self-assessment
- Ability to lighten up (to not take oneself too seriously)

In 2011, the American Society for Training and Development (ASTD), with the assistance of the U.S. Department of Labor, surveyed Fortune 500 firms to determine what skills employers want. Here are the responses, displayed in the order of importance to employers.

THE TEN SKILLS MOST DESIRED IN JOB APPLICANTS BY FORTUNE 500 FIRMS

1. Teamwork
2. Problem-solving skills
3. Interpersonal skills
4. Oral communication skills
5. Listening skills
6. Creative thinking
7. Leadership skills
8. Writing skills
9. Computation skills
10. Reading skills

Still not convinced? In December 2006, Peter D. Hart Research Associates conducted a comprehensive study of employers and recent college graduates for the Association for American Colleges and Universities. The study found that a significant majority of respondents cited skills learned and perfected in networking as the most important skills to look for in new hires. These skills, and the percentage of respondents reporting them as the most important skills, are shown in Figure 1–1. The skills are teamwork (44%), critical thinking (33%), and oral/written communications (30%).

There are scores of other studies that produced similar results. But let's take a step back and apply some common sense to all of these studies. What is it that employers really want in a candidate? The bottom line is that people prefer and want to be around and work with other people whom they know and like. This is not a mystery of the universe or a great discovery of science; it is simply human nature. Think about it and it will make sense. A manager will spend about eight to 10 hours a day with an employee and there will probably be hours of time spent in travel or social time. The manager will want to know that he or she will be able to enjoy this time spent with the employee. In addition, the manager will want to be certain he or she can trust the employee.

Trust and reciprocity are traits and talents people bring with them to the job—they can't be taught. Managers can teach employees the job requirements, but they can't teach new employees to get along with others, to unilaterally find and fix problems, to have good interpersonal skills, to be adaptable to change or uncertainty, or to be willing to take risks.

These kinds of traits and talents are found in people whom managers find from their own networks. If the hiring managers cannot find someone they know and like,

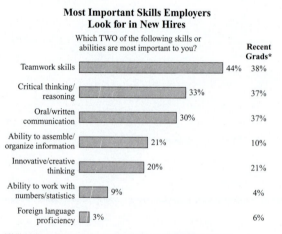

Most Important Skills Employers Look for in New Hires

	Which TWO of the following skills or abilities are most important to you?	Recent Grads*
Teamwork skills	44%	38%
Critical thinking/ reasoning	33%	37%
Oral/written communication	30%	37%
Ability to assemble/ organize information	21%	10%
Innovative/creative thinking	20%	21%
Ability to work with numbers/statistics	9%	4%
Foreign language proficiency	3%	6%

*Skills/abilities recent graduates think are the two most important to employers

Hart, P. D. 2007. *How should colleges prepare students to succeed in today's global economy?* Washington, DC: The Association of American Colleges and Universities, p. 5.

FIGURE 1–1

they will reach out to their personal network of contacts and ask if they know anyone who could fill the position.

People put great stock and trust in their contacts' networks. If their contact knows and likes someone, that candidate has (unbeknownst to them) already made a great first impression on the hiring manager. If the hiring managers cannot find candidates whom they know, or whom a network contact knows, then the traditional job-hunting approaches and tools are put to work to search for prospects with the experience needed who will hopefully become someone the hiring manager will come to know and like.

SO WHAT IS NETWORKING EXACTLY?

Networking isn't supposed to be difficult. In fact, it should just occur naturally. Think about how your relationship with your best friend or significant other developed. You met somewhere, discovered that you shared a common interest, exchanged contact information, and then hung out again. It just sort of happened. You didn't know it, but you were networking. You connected and developed a mutually beneficial relationship with someone. It wasn't an event that you planned. You didn't get out of bed and say, "Today I'm going to make a friend." Networking is something that can happen anywhere. There is no specific time or place. Just like there is no specific time and place to watch your buddy's back. You are continuously doing it.

But let's be honest, networking doesn't come naturally to many people. At first, you may feel like a phony, as if you're trying to "suck up" to people. You may not like the thought of meeting people so you can somehow use them to advance your career. Perhaps the words manipulation and coercion come to mind, along with the notion that people who network are people who get ahead because of *who* they know, not *what* they know. Could it be that you believe there is something inherently sinister, bad, or unfair about leveraging personal contacts to help you get ahead?

You'll soon figure out that networking isn't about finding opportunities for you or "sucking up" to someone in order to get ahead in life. It's about finding opportunities to help others. Remember what we said earlier: Find strength in service. And service is the secret to networking. You want to join as many "squads" as possible rather than trying to find people to join yours. Instead of seeking out and connecting with people who can somehow advance your career, begin looking for people who you are able to help in some way. Helping others is an inherent trait in most veterans. We don't have to think about it, we just do it. If you think of networking as an opportunity to help others, you will naturally develop a network of people who will also have your back.

Here's another way of looking at the process of networking: If you saw an attractive person at a bar, you wouldn't just walk up and ask them to marry you. They'd think you were desperate and it would immediately turn them off. You're much better off playing it cool. You want to walk up to them with some confidence, introduce yourself, and begin a simple conversation to see if there is any chemistry between the two of you. The goal of the conversation is to get their number so you can meet up at a later time, when you have their undivided attention, and can begin to build a relationship.

Networking for professional advancement is exactly the same thing. You wouldn't want to walk right up to someone you didn't know and ask for a job. Just like in dating, there's a courting process involved. When you meet a professional acquaintance, the goal is also to obtain their contact information, in many cases their business card, so you can follow up at a later date, when you have their undivided attention, and can begin to build a professional relationship.

Networking is simply making friends and building trust. That's all it is. If you were given a bunch of free tickets to a Yankee game (okay, some of you would flush them down the toilet, so insert your favorite sports team here), you wouldn't give them away to strangers. You would give them to your friends and family. Why? Because you know that you'd have a good time with them and eventually they'd return the favor. If you gave those tickets to a bunch of strangers, you wouldn't be able to predict whether you'd have a good time or if they'd ever return the favor.

The same exact thing occurs with professional opportunities. When a manager at Company ABC needs to hire an account executive, he or she is first going to see who in their professional network may be interested in the job before telling strangers. Why? It's because they already know and trust the people in their network. Hence they are able to reasonably predict how well someone will perform in the specific position. It reduces the risk and the cost of hiring an incompetent person, just like bringing your friends to a baseball game reduces the risk of having a bad time.

Networking leads to opportunities that most other people normally wouldn't get. It's having the inside track and the ability to get the full and undivided attention of decision makers. Networking gets your foot in the door—it gets you a solid look and maybe even an interview. But remember that it does not get you a job. Do not expect to be given or handed anything just because you know someone. You will still have to make your case, but you've already won half the battle by putting yourself in the position to be considered.

HOW DOES NETWORKING HELP YOU LAND A JOB?

Let's take a look at an example of how people are generally hired at corporations. It's actually not entirely different from how we are processed into the military, except there are no physical fitness tests in corporate America.

Let's say, for example, that the Senior Vice President (SVP) of Advertising Sales at Company ABC wants to grow his business and is looking to hire additional employees. The SVP is equivalent to a full-bird colonel or regimental commander in the infantry. He is extremely busy trying to manage and grow his business, so he doesn't have time to search for candidates, just like regimental commanders don't have time to go to high schools and recruit more soldiers for their units.

Similar to how the military has recruiters and administrative personnel to locate and process new soldiers, the SVP has a Human Resources (HR) Department to search for candidates. The mission of the HR department is to locate qualified applicants based on the hiring criteria given to them by the SVP, conduct initial interviews, whittle the applicant pool down to the best four or five candidates, and then present these candidates to the SVP for the final decision.

This is where many veterans get stuck. The job market is extremely competitive right now. HR personnel have to review dozens and sometimes hundreds of resumes for one position. They only have thirty seconds, at most, to look over a resume and determine whether the person is qualified for the job. And because most HR recruiters haven't served in the military, they don't fully understand our skills and experiences. Therefore, more times than not, our resumes get thrown in the "no" pile and are never considered by the hiring manager.

The trick is to get yourself past HR and in front of a hiring manager (in our example the SVP of Ad Sales)—the decision maker—so that you can verbally make your case for the position. That's our goal! HR personnel can say "no" to a candidate, but they cannot actually hire anyone. That final decision lies with the hiring manager. If a hiring manager already knew you and thought you'd be a strong candidate for a certain position, he would tell HR that he'd be interviewing you, and HR would coordinate and process the appropriate paperwork.

Let's look at this personal example. Last fall Mike was searching for a job. He applied to 34 positions through various companies' online job forums. In 16 of the companies, he was unable to network with a veteran or an employee who worked there. Out of these 16 companies, he received zero callbacks for interviews. In fact, the automatic rejection emails are still trickling in.

For the remaining 18 positions, he was able to connect with a veteran employee at each of the corporations, who was then able to help "refer" or recommend him for the position (we'll talk about how he did this later in the book). Mike ended up getting called back for 10 interviews! Veteran employees conducted two of the interviews and he was subsequently offered positions at both companies. Employees with no military experience conducted his remaining eight interviews, and he only received one offer.

Isn't that amazing? Networking with a veteran employee increased Mike's chances of getting an interview from 0% to over 50%! And both veteran employees who interviewed him subsequently offered him positions at the company.

HOW DOES NETWORKING WITH VETERAN EMPLOYEES INCREASE YOUR CHANCES OF GETTING AN INTERVIEW?

Many firms and organizations are not good at assessing individuals' talents—an applicant's recurring patterns of thought, feelings, actions, and behaviors that naturally equip the individual to excel in a job. Therefore the applicant, using networking and communications skills, has to take charge and be able to demonstrate his or her talents and how he or she will benefit the employer (Gallup, 2009).

What exactly do job applicants have to do? Demonstrate that they will:

1. Reduce the cost of the hire, lower the employee turnover
2. Rate and improve interpersonal relationships with other employees.
3. Adapt quickly to change, be easy to manage, and be quicker to learn roles and therefore have a shorter learning curve.
4. Be more productive, more precise, and more consistent, missing less work, producing higher quality work, making fewer mistakes, reducing management's anxiety and stress, and exceeding expectations.
5. Produce greater customer satisfaction, greater customer retention, and higher profits.

To explain all this and make your case, you need the undivided attention of the decision maker. You can't communicate on your resume that you can do all these things. Let's go back to the main question from our example: Why did networking with veteran employees increase Mike's chances of getting an interview by over 50%? It was because other veterans could adequately assess his military skills and talents. They fully understood his experience and knew that he possessed the interpersonal skills, intellect, and work ethic to excel in the position. He hadn't even met these veterans, but they already were in his professional network and willing to give him a shot because they had served in the military and understood Mike's capabilities. The question now was whether he or she wanted to work with him for eight to 10 hours a day.

Conversely, employees with no military experience could not adequately assess Mike's military skills and experiences, so they were less likely to give him a chance and instead, went with a candidate whose experiences and talents they understood better.

Does all this make sense? If not, go back and re-read this chapter. Understanding why networking is important and knowing the foundational principles of successful networking are crucial to getting the most out of the rest of this book.

SUMMARY

The biggest takeaway from this step is to understand how important networking is for a successful military transition. You can't do it on your own. Ask any veteran who is now in the civilian world and he or she will tell you a story about how someone along the way, usually another veteran, extended a helping hand or provided a crucial introduction that resulted in a job opportunity. Ask for help! You're going to need it.

VETERAN PROFILE

Courtesy of Andrew S. Roberts

NAME: Andrew S. Roberts
TITLE: Director of the Office of Military and Veterans Liaison Services for the North Shore LIJ Health System
SERVICE: United States Army, Iraq Veteran

I served in Iraq as an artillery battery commander. Our mission was turned upside down in 2003 after the initial invasion. My unit ended up providing a wide range of services, from patrols and checkpoints to civil affairs and training the Iraqi security forces. As the enemy activity increased around me, so did my anxiety. By the time I came home a year later, I was suffering from a pretty decent case of post-operational stress, although I didn't quite realize it at the time.

The stress and anxiety that lingered with me after my return didn't exactly help my job search. I was still in somewhat of a combat mode when I got back and I really didn't care what I did for a living. I was just focused on "getting a job." I accepted the first offer from the first company that called me. It was with a homebuilder in California. It was a great company with a lot of room to grow, but I hated it. I quit after six months. I was not fulfilled. I felt I had no purpose, which I have since learned is extremely common among returning veterans.

A year later I moved closer to friends and family in New York, which was helpful for my stress. I was living at home with my mom and dad and realized I really needed to get out of this rut and get my independence back. I still didn't know what I wanted to do, but thought that maybe I could get a job in New York City in commercial construction. So I wrote about 15 letters and sent them to 15 people from construction companies in New York who sounded important (I looked at their websites). I wrote and commented on the specific qualities or projects each company was working on, explained my situation, and asked them for an interview. I also enclosed my resume.

To my surprise, three companies called me, two interviewed me, and two offered me a job. I accepted a position and was really happy to get my independence back. I was working in construction again, but this time working on hospitals. It felt a little more fulfilling; at least this job was going to help people some day. I can admit now though that I knew in my heart this still wasn't the right job for me.

I spent every free minute I had reading about Iraq and Afghanistan. I read the newspapers, watched news shows, and was very interested in government and politics. I thought about it constantly. I felt for the men and women still fighting. I was passionate about the struggles recently returned veterans were having. And in a truly serendipitous moment I learned that the director of a major veterans organization lived on my street in New York City. I called the organization and started volunteering immediately.

It was like true love: "When you know, you know." I knew this was something special. After six months of volunteering, I let them know I was available full time. They interviewed me and then offered me a job at about $20,000 less then what I was currently making. It was a big shock to me. Was I willing to give up a good salary for basically a terrible one, just to do something I cared about?

The answer ended up being yes and I look back at that decision as one of the best I've ever made. The job itself ended up not being the best one for me, but I was now 100% fulfilled and I was in the right field. What a great feeling to wake up every day loving what you do!

As I entered the field of "veterans advocacy" I began interacting with many other people working on similar projects. I worked hard, but I also kept my eyes open. I soon learned there was a job available with the government that was paying nearly $40,000 more than I was currently making, and it was a leadership role as well. It sounded too good to be true. I applied for the position and because I now had relevant experience, I was hired.

My initial cut in pay got me into a field that I love and enabled me to earn a good salary. Since working in this field, I have met many people from a variety of walks of life who all have a shared interest: veterans and their families. I've joined groups and volunteered for causes I care about, all in connection to this cause. The people I've met are my network. They have helped move me ahead in life.

I've since moved on to an even more fulfilling job at an even better salary. There were two keys to this: finding a field I cared about and making connections with others who had the same passion. I made the connections because I wanted to help as many people as I could, and in turn they helped me. They have supported my mission, helped me find new career opportunities, and mentored me to heights I didn't know I could achieve.

PREPARE YOURSELF FOR NETWORKING SITUATIONS

Courtesy of Shutterstock.com

During targeted operations overseas, there were veterans who didn't hesitate at the thought of charging into a building and rooting out a terrorist. But back here at home, some of these same vets are fearful of walking into a room and starting a simple conversation with someone that they don't know. Sounds ridiculous, right? In this chapter, we're going to discuss ways for you to prepare yourself for conversations and networking, so you can minimize the unknown and reduce the anxiety of networking. We're going to provide you with a few simple techniques that will help you expand your comfort zone in order to take advantage of the opportunities at hand.

The difference between charging into a building in Iraq and walking into a room full of people back here at home boils down to one thing: training. For the most part, you were adequately prepared and equipped to conduct targeted operations when you deployed. You trained for months on how to do your job. You could have done it in your sleep. You were almost looking for some action so you could finally put your training to use. When the moment of truth came and you had to charge into that building, or protect your buddy's back, you did it with confidence and without hesitation.

When you leave the military, no one adequately prepares you for this transition. It's a weird feeling to be back in the most familiar place on earth, your hometown, but feel like you no longer belong. Your family and friends are still exactly the same as when you left, but you have changed. You see everything and everyone differently now. It takes some getting used to.

This awkward feeling erodes your confidence, and you're no longer sure how to interact with anyone. All of a sudden, the hard-charging Marine who stormed into buildings dragging out terrorists hesitates at the thought of interacting with others and vying for a job. Why? It's really just a lack of preparation.

Here's another example. Think back to a mission when you had a complete understanding of where you were going, what you were doing, and how to get the heck out of there. Wherever it was, I'm sure there was still a little pucker factor, but you also had a warm and fuzzy feeling because you were prepared and you knew exactly what you had to do. Now think back to a mission when you were not familiar with the area, couldn't really visualize how the mission was going to play out, and didn't have a clear understanding of how to get out of Dodge. (There are probably too many of these missions to choose from, so pick just one.) I bet you were a little anxious, perhaps even a little hesitant to take action during that mission. It's because you weren't adequately prepared.

Now think about a time when you showed up early to a class or an event where there were a few other people already in the room. When you entered, you were faced with the momentary awkwardness of deciding whether to introduce yourself to everyone or sit down in silence alone. What did you do? Did any of these thoughts cross your mind?

- Is it appropriate for me to just walk up and introduce myself? I don't want to interrupt or intrude on their conversation.
- Should I introduce myself to the professor or speaker? I don't want to be seen as a brown-noser.
- What if I'm the new guy and everyone else already knows each other?
- If I do walk up to them, what do I even say? How do I break the ice?

If you've had these thoughts, you're not alone. Most people, particularly veterans, aren't sure what to do in these types of social situations. When you're not familiar with the simple techniques of effective networking, you naturally tend to stay within your comfort zone, and as a result you hesitate. Through preparation, practice, and a little humility, you will be able to have better control of the situation and the conversation, reducing anxiety and achieving the results that you want.

As you read this chapter, think of charging into that building! Let's get started.

THE FIVE STEPS OF NETWORKING

This wouldn't be a book for veterans unless we broke something down into a simple five-step process. Let's take a look at a basic networking example and then examine each step independently to illustrate some of the basic techniques that were used to secure a job interview.

You go to a local watering hole with a few buddies on a Saturday afternoon to watch some college football and drink $3 Bud Light pitchers. During the game, you strike up a conversation with a middle-aged gentlemen sitting next to you at the bar named Andy. You make small talk and chat about the game for a while and then Andy asks you what you do. You tell him that you just got off active duty and you're trying to figure things out. Andy, who is a manager at a large general construction business in town, thanks you for your service and extends his business card. He offers to show you around one of his projects and discuss some career opportunities. You thank him for the offer and agree to reach out to him. The rest of the day you talk sporadically about football and other things. The next day you shoot Andy an email saying that it was a pleasure to meet him and that you're interested in learning more about the employment opportunities at his company. Andy responds in kind.

Over the next few weeks you do some research about Andy's company and compile a list of questions that you want to ask him. You meet him at one of his construction sites and Andy walks you through the building explaining the various intricacies of construction management. He introduces you to employees and asks you some more questions about your skills and experiences.

After an hour or so, Andy has to get back to work. You thank him for his time and guidance. Andy says he wishes he can hire you but unfortunately his budget is pretty tight. However, he's expecting to win a few more contracts in the coming months and if so, he will be looking for some help.

Over the next few months, you keep in touch with Andy. You see him a few more times at the same bar and send him a Merry Christmas email over the holiday season. Four or five months pass and you get a call from Andy. He says a friend of his, who is a manager at a manufacturing company one town over, is looking for a supervisor. Andy thought you'd make a good fit and wants to connect you to his friend. You end up speaking to his friend and he invites you in for a formal interview.

That is how networking works. Let's break this example down into each of its components so you can better understand the process and clearly see what our veteran did correctly to put himself in position to be considered for the supervisor position.

Step 1: Meet People

We'll get more into where you should begin to meet people and the best techniques for "breaking the ice" in future chapters. In our example, you met Andy at a local bar and started a simple conversation with him. That was actually the hard part . . . Good work!

Step 2: Listen and Learn

People love to talk about themselves. All you have to do, really, is just ask the person a few questions about themselves and they will take off with the conversation. You'll also learn more about the person and understand better how you may be able to help them in the future. Think of it as gaining intelligence.

Step 3: Exchange Contact Information

Remember our dating example. The goal of the conversation is to exchange information so you can stay in touch with the person and follow up when you have their undivided attention. You don't have to convince the person that you're awesome right away: Let it marinate.

Step 4: Follow Up

Keep your promises and keep your word. If you promise to do something, do it in a timely manner, even if it's as simple as a "thank you" email or connecting them with another acquaintance. You're showing the person that you are organized, trustworthy, and responsible. In our example, you followed up with Andy and met him at his construction site. He was looking for qualified and hardworking employees, so you were also helping him!

Step 5: Stay in Touch

You're most likely not going to achieve immediate results through networking. It takes some time. Remember, there's a courting process involved. "It's time to start looking for a job, so I better start networking" is the wrong attitude to have. If that's the case, you're already way behind your peers. In our example, you did not achieve the immediate result of landing a job with Andy. But you kept in touch with him for five months and when he heard about an open position with another company, he thought of you and you ended up getting an interview.

This leads us to another great point about "strong" versus "weak" networks. You will actually end up leveraging the most opportunities from your weak network rather than your strong network. Here's why: Your strong network is made up of your closest friends, family members, and co-workers. These are the people that you talk to the most and spend the most time with. As a result, you are all simultaneously privy to the same limited opportunities and information. However, your weak network is comprised of friends and acquaintances you see or speak to sporadically, from once a month to once a year. Maybe your contact is a classmate who you occasionally run into or a former co-worker who left to start his or her own business. These people are exposed to information and opportunities that you and the people in your strong network do not know about. In our example, Andy was someone who was in your weak network. He was a friend, but not someone you would call up or hang out with on a Saturday night. He had information about a job opportunity at a manufacturing company that you or the other members of your strong network did not know about. Does this make sense?

Remember, this five-step system works because it is based on building long lasting relationships. You're not going to get results overnight. If you are patient, trustworthy, and take the initiative to stay in touch with the people in your strong and weak networks, you will put yourself in a position to take advantage of opportunities that others will not get.

BE PREPARED TO TALK ABOUT YOURSELF

You probably hate talking about yourself. In boot camp we were told to remove the word "I" from our vocabulary. But having an effective "personal introduction" is absolutely imperative to leveraging the many contacts and opportunities that will come your way as you make your transition out of the military.

When you leave active duty, you have a very short window of opportunity during which people are willing to help you. It is understood among the majority of Americans that making the transition from the military to the civilian world is very challenging. If you introduce yourself as a recently transitioned veteran, people are going to take a little extra interest in you. This is your opportunity to make some great connections, but remember that these opportunities won't last forever. The longer that you've been off active duty, the less people are willing to help you.

Your short personal introduction is the key to unleashing the potential that can come from each contact. The key is to make it extremely easy for the person to understand where you've been, what you want to do, and determine how they can help you.

The personal introduction is broken down into two basic parts: what you've done and what you want to do.

For part one, you should summarize your military experiences in one or two sentences and also be sure to mention that you are a transitioning service member. Here are some examples:

- "I'm a former Marine sergeant who transitioned off active duty a few months ago."
- "I joined the Army after the 9/11 attacks and deployed several times over to Iraq and Afghanistan. After my third deployment I left active duty, which was about a year ago."

These are extremely basic summaries of your military experiences, but remember that civilians won't understand military occupations, names of operations, or what personal awards mean. Plus you're just meeting the person, so you need to keep it short and to the point. You simply want to let them know which branch of service you were in, any deployments to Iraq or Afghanistan (it's your choice whether you want to say this), and when you transitioned off active duty. If they are interested in learning more about you, they will ask a follow-up question, which you can then answer specifically.

Part two is much more difficult to master than part one. Think of it this way: Part one is the "hook" or the way you are going to get people interested in helping you. Part two is when you "sink" the hook and explain how people can help you. You want to communicate specifically where you want to go but also leave yourself open to other opportunities. Clear as mud, right?

Here's another way of looking at it. A little kid comes to you crying and you ask him, "What's the matter?" If he can't tell you, how are you going to help him? You can't until he describes to you what's wrong, right? The same goes for professional conversations. If you say to someone, "I don't know what I want to do," or if you can't communicate in a clear way how someone can provide you assistance, then how can that person help you?

Now, many of you have absolutely no idea what you want to do. Welcome to the club. Hardly anyone transitioning off active duty knows exactly what he or she wants to do. If you don't have a specific job function or company in mind, use your geographic location preference or specific skill sets that you possess to show some focus. People want to help people who know how to help themselves. Check out some examples below:

- "I'm currently majoring in finance at Baruch College. I'm most interested in getting into private wealth management, however I'm certainly open to exploring other areas of finance."
- "I really don't know what I want to do. I'm currently exploring several different opportunities, however I do know that I want to stay in the local area."
- "I'm still trying to figure out exactly what I want to do. I was a logistics manager in the Navy, so I'm currently looking at some positions where those skills will translate."

Here are parts one and two put together:

- "I'm a former Marine sergeant who transitioned off active duty a few months ago. I'm currently majoring in finance at Baruch College and I'm looking to get into private wealth management, however I'm certainly open to exploring other areas of finance as well."
- "I joined the Army after the 9/11 attacks and deployed several times over to Iraq and Afghanistan. After my third deployment I left active duty, which was about a year ago. I really don't know what I want to do. I'm currently exploring several different opportunities, however I do know that I want to stay in the local area."

That's all there is to it. It's a very clear and concise personal introduction of what you've done and where you want to go. If the person is interested in learning more about you, they will ask follow-up questions that you can answer specifically.

BE CAREFUL USING "MILITARY SPEAK" AROUND CIVILIANS

The military has a language all its own. We swear, have acronyms for everything, and refer to everyday items by different names, likes heads, go-fasters, ink-sticks, and portholes. We can barely understand each other, so there's absolutely no way a civilian will understand what we're saying. The following is a list of some things you should be aware of when speaking to non-veterans. A general rule of thumb is to speak to everyone as if you were speaking to your mother or father.

- If you call a man "sir" and he tells you to call him by his first name, do not continue to call him "sir." It doesn't matter how old he is or what his occupation is. If he says, "Call me Jim," then call him Jim.
- Under no circumstances do you ever, ever, ever, ever, ever call a woman "ma'am." Just don't do it. Calling a woman "ma'am" makes her feel old. Call women by their first names or use "Mrs. or "Ms."
- Do not use acronyms. If a civilian asks you what you did in the military, don't respond like this: "I was an infantry squad leader for 1st Platoon, Lima 3/3 and also served as a range coach for Weapons and Training Battalion. Ended up doing a pump to the 'Ghan and a UDP to Oki. EAS'd about a year ago." They will have absolutely no idea what you're talking about. By using acronyms or terminology that others don't know, you make them feel stupid, which is the opposite effect that you want to have on people.
- Stop calling bathrooms the head or latrine. A wall is no longer a bulkhead; a floor is not the deck; sneakers aren't go-fasters; pens are no longer ink-sticks.
- Don't wear platoon t-shirts with any type of bloody skulls or "death/killing quotes" to class or other social functions. These types of t-shirts help build camaraderie and unit cohesion in the military, but they are not appropriate to wear around civilians who did not go through what we all did.
- Speaking loud is no longer a testament to your leadership abilities. It's actually very scary to civilians. Speak in a conversational tone.
- Sometimes veterans also "overcompensate" and act too familiar with civilians in professional settings to show that they are able to communicate or interact in a non-military way. "Hey man, what's up?" is not an appropriate way to greet a potential boss or professional colleague. Remember, your boss or colleagues in the civilian world are not your friends. Don't speak to them or treat them as if they are.

SHOULD YOU TELL WAR STORIES?

Yes and no. First, a common question you will receive from your friends or peers when you come home will be whether you killed anyone. Regardless of whether you have, it's no one's business—this is a very personal question. A great response is, "Fortunately no." No good comes from you sharing war stories about killing the Taliban, so why even go there? You have nothing to prove to anyone back home. Be prepared, because you will get this question and you need to know how you're going to answer it.

When you go into a job interview and you are being asked questions by someone who has never served in the military, it's incumbent upon you to make the interviewer feel comfortable asking you questions about your overseas experiences. For most of us, our experiences in Iraq and Afghanistan truly define who we are today as a leader and professional. You have to be able to explain how the experience acquired overseas will help you be the best possible employee if you want to get hired.

You can only do this by explaining your experience overseas in a way that the interviewer is comfortable hearing. In nearly every interview that you go into, the interviewer is going to ask you an open-ended question about you or your military experiences, such as "Tell me about yourself," "Tell me about your experiences in the Army," or "Give me an example of a time when you led a team."

This is your opportunity to explain what you did in the military on your terms and to open the conversation up for the interviewer to better understand your skills and experiences. If you don't, and you leave the interview without giving the hiring manager a clear idea of what you're capable of, you won't be hired.

Let's say you deployed to Afghanistan as an infantry team leader and were in charge of three other soldiers. You could say, "I was an infantry fire team leader in charge of three other soldiers in Afghanistan. I led them on over 100 combat patrols that contributed to the neutralization of an estimated 200-person enemy force in Kunar Province. As a result, attacks in our province were reduced by over 40% during our time there."

What follow-up question is the interviewer going to ask you now about your experience in the military? After an answer like that, they will move on without really understanding what you did or how you performed.

You can say something like this to make the interviewer more comfortable asking follow-up questions:

"I was directly responsible for leading three other soldiers during a year-long deployment to Afghanistan. This encompassed everything, including their training, equipment, professional development, and safety. On a day-to-day basis, we worked with the Afghan police to conduct security operations in a mid-sized city, helping to bring safety to a population of over 100,000 people. We helped train the Afghan police, we provided security and transportation to medical doctors to remote villages, and also provided additional security measures for government agencies so they could implement work programs to unemployed citizens."

Do you see the difference? There are many follow-up questions that the interviewer can derive from this response and, more importantly, feel comfortable doing so. Focus your stories and experiences on the positive aspects of your deployments, particularly when you are vying for a job. It will make the interviewer feel more comfortable asking follow-up questions and give them a better understanding of what you are capable of, which gives you a better chance of being hired.

GIVE YOURSELF PERMISSION

Give yourself permission to network. This may sound really stupid to you. But mentally preparing yourself and having a positive attitude is imperative to taking that first step. Just allowing that "switch" in your mindset can make all the difference. It's sort of like that "game-time" switch you turn on before a big football game or before stepping into a helicopter for an important mission. If you tell yourself you can do it, then you will.

HAVE A BUSINESS CARD

Business cards are absolutely necessary for networking. You don't need to have a job or a business in order to have a business card. If you want a person to remember you or to contact you, a business card is a must. There are many online services such as Vista.com, overnightprints.com, 123print.com, and printcentric.com that produce a limited number of business cards for free or for an inexpensive fee. In addition, Microsoft and other software programs can produce perfectly acceptable business cards that you can print on your own computer. Lastly, FedEx shipping stores, Office Depot, and Staples can print small quantities of cards (250–500) for under $40.

As a veteran, all you really need to have on your business card is your name, phone number, email address, and branch of service. You can certainly add your rank and military specialty or billet as well. Ensure you use a professional email address that is comprised of some combination of your name or initials. For example: michael.abrams@gmail.com or m.abrams@hotmail.com. Save usmcgrunt0311@yahoo.com and kingofbattle69@gmail.com for your friends.

When ending a conversation, it's also perfectly appropriate to ask someone for his or her business card. Think of it like asking another veteran which unit they were with. You can say, for instance, "It was really great meeting you, Amanda, do you have a business card? I'd like to stay in touch with you." It's as simple as that.

A WARM SMILE IS BETTER THAN A GREAT OPENING LINE

A natural, comfortable, and warm smile with a firm handshake is better than the greatest opening line of all time. Most human communication is actually non-verbal. This simply means that your initial contact and subsequent follow-up communication with another person will be predominantly conducted through body language and tone.

You don't have to come up with an insightful or funny opening line that will immediately impress people. What veterans in particular have to focus on is smiling. Yes, smiling. Veterans have a tendency to look serious or even mean, particularly when we're in an uncomfortable or "hostile" situation, like when we're faced with networking. If someone thinks you're angry, it doesn't matter what you say, that person will be reluctant to have a conversation with you. Focus on having a friendly demeanor and presenting yourself with a humble confidence instead of coming up with a perfect opening line,

Although a nice smile and a firm handshake are the most important things when meeting someone, it would be a little weird if you just stood there and didn't say anything. The idea is to have your opening line support your friendly and confident demeanor—something that is normal, disarming, and conversational given the situation and does not sound not awkwardly rehearsed. Remember, this isn't rocket science, so don't over think things. Here are a few ideas that you can customize:

- "Hi, my name is Mike. It's nice to meet you."

This is by far the best way to introduce you to anyone. It's simple, straightforward, disarming, and can be used in just about every situation. You can use this introduction as a lead-in to all of the follow-up questions listed here:

- "I'm a student here at NYU," or "I was in the Army and now I'm transitioning off active duty. What do you do?"
- "What brought you out to this luncheon?"
- "Have you attended this type of event before? What do you think of it?"
- "Are you a member? I'm thinking of joining this organization as well."
- "How have you found these events?
- "I'm new here. Can you tell me something about this group?"

Please note that you want to ask "open-ended" questions when you're first meeting someone and trying to start a conversation. These are questions that require more than a one- or two- word answer. The trick is to get the other person to talk about him or herself. Remember, you're trying to gain some "intel" so you can get to know the person better, so get that person talking!

DO YOUR RESEARCH AND KNOW SOMETHING ABOUT THE PEOPLE YOU'RE MEETING

If you were successful networking with another veteran and have set up a time to grab a few beers with him or her to continue your conversation, research the person and his or her company or organization. Find out as much information as possible about him or her as well as the company. Check out the company's website and LinkedIn profile, Google the company, and also look for recent press or articles.

Keep in mind that you are searching for any and all ways to differentiate yourself from every other contact your associate meets. Any piece of information you have that shows your interest, knowledge, or initiative in this person's field begins to create a rapport and could lead to the individual building an interest in you.

HAVE A LIST OF "GET-TO-KNOW-YOU" QUESTIONS PREPARED

Get-to-know-you questions are different from your opening statement or introduction in that they focus on the person with whom you are speaking, not an event you both may be attending or a situation you both may be experiencing. It's good to have a few of these questions rehearsed and ready for when you unexpectedly meet someone. These questions can relate to family, travel, hobbies, favorite books, movies, and other interests. Here are a few examples:

- "Where do you work and what do you do?"
- "Where do you live?"
- "What are you majoring in?"
- "What unit were you with?" (For veterans)
- "What do you do when you're not working?"

WEAR A LAPEL PIN

A military lapel pin may be the best $8 investment of your life. A lapel pin is a very small and discreet pin that connects to the upper left portion of your business jacket's lapel. If you begin to look for it, you'll see that a lot of veterans wear one, which displays their branch of service or even a particular unit. It is an absolutely great conversation starter and you'll be surprised how many people will approach you because of it. Get one immediately, if not sooner!

HAVE AN EXIT STRATEGY AND FOLLOW-UP PLAN

Even when you are engaged in a great conversation with someone, it is perfectly polite to leave something for the next time and close your conversation with a follow-up plan in order to move on and talk with someone else. Or maybe you just can't stand the person you're talking to; we've all been there. The point is to break contact respectfully and leave the door open for future engagement. Here are some lines to practice:

- "It was great meeting you and hopefully we can continue our conversation some other time."
- "Thanks for sharing the information about your 'Jump-to-Conclusions Door Mat.' It sounds exciting. Best of continued success."
- "Please excuse me, I want to catch my friend before she leaves."
- "I enjoyed hearing about your experiences in the first Gulf War. Can I buy you a beer a little later?"

If it's appropriate and you'd like to stay in touch with the person, don't forget to ask for his or her business card and follow up. A simple email the following day is the quickest and easiest way to set up a follow-up meeting. Here is an example:

Hi Jim,

It was great meeting you last night. I'm sure you're busy, however if you can escape work sometime in the next few weeks I'd like to grab a drink and hear more about what you do at Turner Construction. It's a career path that I'm very interested in. Have a great week and I look forward to your reply.

Respectfully,
Mike

SUMMARY

These simple networking principles will help you better prepare yourself to get through awkward networking moments with confidence. Once you start practicing and applying them, you will find yourself actually enjoying meeting new people and charging into social situations.

VETERAN PROFILE

NAME:	Jesse Friszell
TITLE:	Columbia University Student and Goldman Sachs Operations Intern
SERVICE:	United States Army, Iraq Veteran

Courtesy of Jesse Friszell

There are few things a soldier with a head of steam and a map can't accomplish. If you tell him to take that house over yonder, he will. If you tell him to train his fellow soldiers, he will. If you tell him to clean the entire armory, he'll grumble, but he will. He'll use his head, he'll use his body, and he'll use whatever resources are available to complete the objective and move on to the next one. He'll analyze, differentiate, classify, and delegate tasks to his subordinates and he'll supervise each one of them, allowing nothing to fall through the cracks. He'll think around problems, motivate his soldiers, and utilize his training in order to navigate whatever obstacle stands between him and his objective. A soldier doesn't just think about problems, he thinks through them. His training beats into him that a mindless soldier is a dead soldier. This mentality, that anything is possible, is the concrete foundation of his personality. A soldier isn't just a pair of hands—he's an asset.

For all its benefits, this kind of mentality can be a disadvantage during the transition from the military to civilian life. When I left the Army in 2007, I felt there was literally nothing I couldn't accomplish. For an entire year I was trained for combat in Korea, and during the following year, I refined that training with real life experience in Iraq. I spent my remaining time in Ft. Carson, doing my best to pass on what I had learned to a new generation of soldiers guaranteed to spend some time in the desert. My subordinates and my superiors alike valued my experience. I was trusted with responsibilities that no 20-year-old kid would ever be entrusted with in the civilian world. Decorated combat veterans, both enlisted men and officers, respected me and listened to what I had to say.

When I left the Army I was 21 years old, but I did not feel 21. I had lived what I felt like to be about 10 or 15 years between 2003 and 2007. I looked and presented myself differently from my college-educated peers, who looked as if they had been at Spring Break in Cancun for the last four years. I knew at the bottom of my heart that once an employer saw me, he would hire me. There was *no way* that if given a choice, he would choose some kid who had sat in a classroom for a couple years over me. I was wrong.

I never even had a chance. My resume looked like crap, and I had no idea how to make it look any better. On top of that, I didn't know anyone. My job search consisted of driving around town with my ugly resume or trolling the Internet. I didn't know if I was overqualified or underqualified for the positions I was applying for, and it was months before I got my first interview. It was for a "manager" position at a local rent-to-own chain, and I nailed the interview (Thank you, NCO promotion boards). I got the job, but quit on my first day. Their business plan was to just "take advantage of low-income people." After four years of being proud of where I worked, I was not prepared to accept a job like that.

Looking back now, it was like I was just feeling around in the dark, hoping to get lucky. Chances are, if I knew what I know now, that even without a degree I would have been able to land a solid job. My transition was a nightmare, because I just wasn't prepared to take a few steps back in order to take a leap forward. I thought my military training had prepared me for everything that life could throw my way, but it hadn't. Not by a long shot. It takes more than a good-looking suit and a decent smile to get a job. The biggest hurdle is being considered in the first place. I knew in the marrow of my bones that I would be an asset to any company that hired me, but I didn't know how to express that, or even whom to express that to. The military doesn't train you how to sell yourself, like you have to everyday in the civilian world. But luckily the Army taught me how to learn. Now that I know what I'm doing, anything is possible—just like when I was wearing the uniform.

Courtesy of Shutterstock.com

BEGIN MAKING CONNECTIONS

The military community is completely removed from the civilian world. After serving a few tours, it can feel like you've been living on a deserted island somewhere, and some of you literally were. The Internet helps keep you connected to your friends and family, but it can still feel like you don't know anyone as you make your transition back home. In this step, we discuss where you can begin making connections that will help you make a successful military transition.

You are already a member of the strongest network of people in the world: veterans of the U.S. military. We know the last thing you want to do when you transition out of the military is hang out with other veterans—we all go through that phase.

Get this feeling out of your system as quickly as possible: Go relax somewhere, get "nasty" and grow your hair out, and get away from everything military. When you run out of money and you're faced with the prospect of living with your parents again, leveraging the veteran contacts in your community won't seem so bad.

Where do you begin? Most veterans who transition off active duty have absolutely no idea what they want to do. If you feel this way, welcome to the club. Start by exploring all the different careers and opportunities that are out there by connecting and speaking with the people who are closest to you. Try to meet as many new people as possible too. Be a sponge. Take in as much as possible so you can begin to target your networking to specific people and companies. When you first start, you'll probably learn more about what you don't want to do than exactly what you do want to do. That's okay! At least you're narrowing down your options.

NETWORK WITH YOUR FRIENDS AND FAMILY

This sounds like a given, but it's surprising how reluctant some people can be to ask family for help. Talk to your mother and father; ask them about their career paths. See if they know anyone who's hiring. If you have any siblings or aunts and uncles, do the same. Reconnect with your old high school friends as well. See what they're doing and whether they like their current career paths. If nothing else, you'll learn about a career or industry and realize that you absolutely do not want to pursue it.

STAY CONNECTED WITH THE VETERANS YOU SERVED WITH

Be proactive and stay connected with the men and women who you served with on active duty. Whether it's through Facebook, LinkedIn, email, or another mode, make sure that they are permanently in your world in some way and that you're doing everything you can to help and support them in their transitions.

As you and your veteran buddies establish yourselves professionally and begin to advance in your careers, you will all rise and mutually support one another along the way, just as if you were on patrol overseas. Remember, we may lose our rank when we exit the military, but we never lose our commitment to watching each other's backs. Reach out and reconnect with your platoon commander, first sergeant, squad leader, and even the greenest boot in your unit—you never know where your next opportunity will come from.

You should also connect with the veteran support groups in your community. If you're in school, by far the best veteran support group to become an active member in is your university's student veteran's club. These are veterans just like you. They are experiencing the same difficulties, thoughts, and feelings that you are having. It is an unbelievable support network, and these veterans will most likely begin new careers in the same city or town as you. You may end up working with or establishing friendships with these veterans for decades to come. Similar to the veterans who you served with on active duty, this is another group of veterans who you can mutually support and grow your career with.

A few other veteran support groups that you can connect with are the American Legion, Veterans of Foreign Wars, and the Marine Corps League. Again, we know the last place you want to go on a Friday night is the local VFW, so don't—go on a Tuesday night instead. Show your face and let the veterans in your community know who you are. These veterans know what you're going through. They've been there and are not only in a position to potentially help you, but they *want* to help you.

In fact, the reason this book was written is because of a relationship that started from attending a local American Legion monthly meeting one night. Mike sat next to an Army veteran, Rick Miners, who is a retired executive recruiter, entrepreneur, and published author. They struck up a conversation, exchanged contact information, and ended up meeting for lunch a few weeks later. After lunch Rick connected Mike to Andrea, and several months after that, this book was published. It's incredible that the opportunity to write this book came from Mike stopping by the American Legion after working out one night. But that's how it happens! There are a lot of veteran organizations out there: Iraq and Afghanistan Veterans of America, Student Veterans of America, American Women Veterans. Take advantage of all of them as you make your transition.

VOLUNTEER WITH A LOCAL NON-PROFIT ORGANIZATION

This will help expand your network and give you some valuable civilian experience to put on your resume. When Mike first came to New York City, he volunteered with an organization called Reserve Aid, which provides financial assistance to wounded service members. One of his veteran buddies was on the board of directors, so Mike followed him to a meeting one night, sat in the back, and just did whatever was asked of him, which wasn't much, but he was happy to just be there and help out. Mike ended up getting a lot back in return. He met countless other veterans and influential people in the New York City area. His network nearly doubled in size. And it just so happened that the founder of the organization was a graduate of New York University and a former Army tanker. He ended up writing Mike's graduate school application recommendation for NYU.

In short, go volunteer someplace. It won't kill you to give up a few hours of your time a month. There are so many great organizations out there that help veterans, underprivileged children, the homeless, and other groups in need. Find a way to give to your community. You will end up getting so much back in return.

SUMMARY

You are a member of the strongest network of people in the world. You have more contacts and opportunities than you think. But it's on you to find and take advantage of them!

VETERAN PROFILE

Courtesy of Lauren Schulz

NAME:	Lauren Schulz
TITLE:	Columbia University Graduate Student
SERVICE:	United States Marine Corps, Iraq Veteran

The majority of my adult life has been dedicated to serving in the United States Marine Corps. The dedication and Esprit de Corp of a Marine cannot be measured and is rarely understood. Because of this, the decision to join paled in comparison to the difficult decision to leave. But in 2008, after six years of serving at home and abroad, I found myself signing my last set of orders and walking away with my DD214. I was excited about what the future had in store for me and felt confident that the next chapter of my life was going to be as good as the last.

I had just finished 12 months in Iraq serving alongside a community of brave men and women. I was the senior air director in al Anbar and was trained to direct aviation operations for the province. I trained for years and had to achieve numerous qualifications for this position. I was proud when I finally reached this level and was able to lead a team of highly qualified and dedicated Marines. Each step of the way I had the support of amazing men and women—nothing I accomplished was done on my own.

As one part of the job, my unit answered requests daily to evacuate injured Marines from the battlefield with our aircraft. It was our job to ensure this was done as quickly and safely as possible. Our team worked in unison, knowing that this was our brother or sister, sometimes fighting for their life, on the other end. We accomplished hundreds of these missions and rarely knew the name of the Marine under our care. When the situations were tense and the odds seemed stacked against the success of the mission, the Marines around me would rise to the occasion and prevail under pressure. I feel privileged to have participated in these operations and they are the proudest moments of my life. With these experiences under my belt, I thought I could do anything, including something simple like finding a job. I was mistaken.

Less than a year later, I was living in my parents' apartment in New York City and filing for unemployment. I was 28 years old, had a college degree, and incredible experience and training, but I felt completely lost. I had no idea what to do or where to look. It took some time, but I finally realized what should have been obvious. As a Marine, any success I had was because amazing, driven, dedicated people surrounded me. We supported each other every step of the way. So I started my search, not for a job, but for other veterans like the ones I had the honor to serve with previously.

In a matter of days, I had reached out to a few Marines and already felt my motivation returning. I realized I was part of an incredible network that reached deep into a wide array of careers throughout the city. Just like serving on active duty, there was a massive team of people just like me who were willing to help. I didn't get through basic training or deployments on my own and I came to find out that I didn't need to get through a career change on my own either.

Through LinkedIn I reached out to one particular Marine veteran named Dan, who agreed to meet me the following day for coffee. He introduced me to a dozen other veterans and helped me get my life back on track. I have since joined the reserves, am in my last semester of graduate school at Columbia University, and certainly don't have to live with my parents anymore.

Dan and I never served together on active duty, nor have most of the veterans I have since met, but we share a common bond that doesn't break once we retire the uniform. The network is out there, already established. I am honored to be part of it and feel that it is now my duty to represent those in uniform in the civilian world, serve them proud, and help others make the transition to civilian life.

Courtesy of Scott Olson / Getty Images, Inc.

CHARACTERISTICS OF GREAT NETWORKERS

Do you know someone who can walk into a room full of strangers and immediately make friends? Can you recall someone who instantly made you feel at ease when you first met him or her? How about a person who makes you feel as though YOU are the only person in the world when they are speaking to you? In this step we discuss the characteristics of great networkers and how you can develop these same traits to become a great networker too.

LEADERSHIP TRAITS

Take a moment to think about some personality traits that great networkers possess. Some of these may come to mind: Bearing, Tact, Unselfishness, Initiative, Enthusiasm, and Courage (see Table 4–1). Do these traits sound familiar to you? In the military, we call these characteristics "leadership traits." These leadership traits, the same ones your first sergeant reminded you of every time you got into trouble, are also the characteristics of great networkers on the civilian side. As a transitioning veteran, you already possess the potential to become a great networker; you just have to tailor your leadership traits to a different type of battlefield.

TABLE 4–1. Leadership Traits of Great Networkers

Traits	Military Description
Bearing	The way you conduct and carry yourself. Your manner should reflect alertness, competence, confidence, and control.
Tact	Deal with people in a manner that will maintain good relations and avoid problems. This means that you are polite, calm, and firm.
Unselfishness	Avoid making yourself comfortable at the expense of others. Be considerate of others. Give credit to those who deserve it.
Initiative	Take action even though you haven't been given orders. This means meeting new and unexpected situations with prompt action. It includes using resourcefulness to get something done without the normal material or methods available to you.
Enthusiasm	A sincere interest and exuberance in the performance of your duties. If you are enthusiastic, you are optimistic, cheerful, and willing to accept the challenges.
Courage	Courage allows you to remain calm while recognizing fear. Moral courage means having the inner strength to stand up for what is right and to accept blame when something is your fault. Physical courage means that you can continue to function effectively when there is physical danger present.

Civilian Translations
Bearing

Bearing is confidence. It's having a presence. Think back to your drill instructors. They are the perfect example of military bearing. But their confidence didn't develop overnight. It came with experience and grew over time. Just like the way your bearing and confidence grew as you gained experience in the military. Remember how difficult it was for you initially to give your drill instructors the morning report? Did you also notice that as you gained experience, not only did these seemingly difficult tasks get much easier, but also other soldiers were more interested in what you had to say? As you gained experience and confidence it was suddenly much easier to have an influence on operations and expand your network.

Coming out of the military, you already have a strong foundation of confidence; you just need to improvise and adapt it to the civilian world. Think of it as "renovating" or "updating" your military bearing to meet the challenges of the civilian world.

How do you do that? You have to step out of your comfort zone and take some risks. It helps to start small (just like in boot camp) and then build from each new experience. If you're a college student, almost every university has a student activity department that oversees student clubs, organizations, and other events in which you can become involved. Here you can begin the small steps of updating your bearing in a civilian environment. A great place to start is your university's student veteran's club. If your college doesn't have one, start one up.

If you're not a student, there are plenty of organizations or non-profits that you can join in your community. Try starting with your local veteran support organizations and go from there.

Tact

Tact is the act of understanding how to effectively communicate with other people. Think back to your pre-deployment training. Many of you probably attended cultural classes to learn about the customs and courtesies of the Iraqi or Afghan people. You had to learn about the culture to effectively communicate with the local people. You may have learned the local language, basic courtesies, how to show respect, what to say and what not to say, and a host of other things. In other words, you learned how to be tactful.

There are many cultural differences between the military and corporate worlds. You can't treat your co-workers the same way you treated your troops. And talking to your boss with a dip in is no longer appropriate either. In a later chapter we discuss some more mistakes in tact that veterans typically make.

Unselfishness

No one understands unselfishness better than a veteran. The mere fact that you joined the armed forces during a time of war shows that you have the inherent ability to put others before yourself. Remember what we talked about before: The key to networking is not to get people to do things for you or to "join" your team. The key is to help as many people as possible, whether it's connecting them with others in your network, giving a little of your time, or providing assistance to them in some other small way. You want to position yourself as the person that people come to when they need help, not the other way around.

Initiative

Initiative may be the most important quality you can have in the civilian world. Once you're handed your DD-214, no one is going to tell you what to do anymore. There's no more reveille, formations, or a sergeant to tell you what the plan of the day is going to be. Some of you are probably saying "Thank God," but it's a double-edged sword. Now you're responsible for figuring it all out yourself.

Abraham Lincoln once said that, "Good things come to those who wait, but only the things left over by those who hustle." This couldn't be truer, especially as it pertains to networking. A great networker is always looking for opportunities to help and connect others. He or she doesn't wait for others to contact them or ask for help. You were taught to never volunteer for anything in the military, but in the civilian world, you should be volunteering for EVERYTHING! Don't just ask to help, go help! Don't just give out your business card, ask for someone's contact information and follow up with the person! Don't expect anyone to help you or hold your hand. You have to take the lead.

Enthusiasm

No one wants to be around a boring person. People want to be around others who are positive and who make them feel better about themselves. In the military, showing emotion is considered weak. We are supposed to maintain an "even keel" demeanor at all times. And with good reason: We don't want people who freak out under fire. We want people who remain calm and can think clearly under the direst circumstances.

But in the civilian world, this demeanor can come across as boring or even a little creepy. It's okay to show emotion and to be passionate about something. It will only draw more people to you and provide you with more opportunities to help others and meet new people. Smiling should be your default face!

Courage

Without courage, you can't network. It's as simple as that. It's amazing how Marines and soldiers will run without hesitation toward the sound of gunfire. And it's equally amazing how hardened, combat veterans are paralyzed with fear at the thought of walking up to someone they don't know and starting a simple conversation.

We had a saying on recruiting duty: You have to get the "no's" if you want to get the "yes's." This means that you're not going to be successful in everything you do. You will fail. You will embarrass yourself. But at least you had the courage to put yourself out there. And if you continue to put yourself out there, you will ultimately succeed in whatever you choose to do. If you're not failing, you're not trying.

Ask yourself, "What's the worst thing that can possibly happen?" Is an Iraq combat veteran really afraid of someone telling them no? It sounds ridiculous. But some people are paralyzed with fear when placed in certain social situations. If you are one of these people, it's okay; we all have varying levels of anxiety in social situations. Experienced networkers and public speakers just know how to handle the fear and turn it into positive energy and enthusiasm. Remember what we said earlier in the chapter—baby steps. Start small with your university's veterans club and practice meeting new, likeminded people. Begin to renovate and rebuild your bearing, confidence, and courage. The next thing you know you'll feel like that salty sergeant running the platoon again.

VETERAN PROFILE

NAME:	Gerry Byrne
TITLE:	Media and Communications Executive, Penske Media Corporation
SERVICE:	United States Marine Corps, Vietnam 1968–1969

Courtesy of Gerry Byrne

I returned from Vietnam in early 1969 after my 13-month tour and released from active duty shortly thereafter. I was proud of my accomplishments but oddly troubled, empty, and confused. "Welcome home" was solely a family affair, not the country's "thank you for your service" that was at least a dream we all hoped would await our return. I was discharged and dropped off of a cliff into a world I didn't know or like and that certainly didn't know or care about me. I was angry and depressed and hated not being understood. And I felt no one cared. One day I was leading Marines in Vietnam, then nothing. I was also three years behind those who didn't serve whose careers were at least gaining traction.

Vietnam was a negative subject that was not high on anyone's chat list other than occasional cocktail comments I'd overhear asking why anyone in their right mind would volunteer to go. "Right mind" was beginning to bother and scare me. Where was I? Who was I? What value did I bring to anyone? These are vivid feelings I can resurrect as if it were yesterday. In college I was an economics major with an intense ambition to enter the world of corporate finance following my three years in the Corps. But with 1969's Wall Street in turmoil and avails in training programs few and far between, even that hunt dragged me more deeply into a dangerous depression.

Then suddenly the "turmoil" did me a positive turn. A "sales and marketing development" role became available at *The New York Daily News*. What did I know about advertising and media sales? Nothing. But newspaper publishing and the mayhem of Madison Avenue was "sold" to me by a group of senior news executives who saw me as one of them. They were vets. These Marine, Navy, and Army combat veterans from Korea and World War II recognized me as an experienced leader with integrity, discipline, and work habits that would be valuable resources for the news. They saved me. There brought me into their family and made me feel at home. My fellow veterans saved me. I will never forget that. And I also never forget the resurrected pride I had as an American, a veteran, and a Marine.

Over the years I've had the good fortune to progress and grow in my media career, always remembering how close I was to a crash but most importantly remembering that it was my fellow vets who provided the guiding light. It is an obligation that I feel I must return. Every day.

Today I'm a proud and active trustee of the Intrepid Museum, the Fisher House Foundation, the Bob Woodruff Foundation, the Veterans Healing

Initiative, and Veterans Advantage. Whether it's honoring and respecting military history, supporting our brave warriors and their families during hospitalization, raising awareness for the devastating impact of traumatic brain injury and post-traumatic stress, addressing complex issues surrounding drug and alcohol abuse, or providing veteran's member discounts on brands that include Ford, Apple, and Amtrak, it's never enough when it comes to supporting our veterans.

I remember a young Marine Sergeant I met in 1969 who, after lighting my cigarette, showed me the inscription on his lighter: "For those who have fought for it, Freedom has a taste that the protected will never know." That says it all.

Courtesy of Shutterstock.com

TARGET THE RIGHT PEOPLE

Once you have a good idea of what you want to do, how do you focus your networking efforts on getting an interview with a specific company? In this step, we discuss a simple process to systematically network your way into a company in order to land an interview and give yourself the best possible chance at beginning a new career of your choosing.

A common mistake that many veterans make is that they apply to just three or four jobs and figure they will get an offer from one of them. This is no longer the case in today's competitive job market. A realistic number is more like 20 to 30 applications in order to receive one or two offers. The hiring process at corporations typically takes months and a lot can happen within that timeframe that's out of your control: hiring freezes, acquisitions, other employees leave or get shifted around. You cannot rely on applying to only a few jobs. You have to cast a wide net!

This past year, Mike was part of an organization, called Four Block, which provided professional development to a group of 16 student veterans in the New York City area.

The goal of this program was to teach these student veterans how to network, provide networking opportunities at large corporations, and then assist them in applying for internships at major Fortune 500 companies. To date, 14 of the 16 student veterans have been successful in landing very competitive summer internships at companies like AT&T, Goldman Sachs, JPMorgan Chase, CitiGroup, and NBCUniversal.

Their success was due in large part to the meticulous way the student veterans adhered to their individual internship attack plans, and their understanding that applying online wasn't effective; they had to get out from behind their computers and build relationships with veteran employees who worked at the companies at which they were applying.

Let's take a look at what they did.

STEP 1: CREATE AN INITIAL TARGET LIST

For the purposes of this book, we're going to start with targeting 15 different companies. Realistically, you should start with at least 30, but it's up to you. Several student veterans in the Four Block program ended up targeting 40 to 50 companies.

- The first five companies are your "selected companies." These are companies that you would absolutely love to work for. Whether it's Google, AT&T, Coors Brewing Company, the local police department, or somewhere else, list out these companies regardless of whether you believe you are capable of getting a job there.
- For the next five, list companies in which you already know someone who works there, whether it's a family member, a veteran that you served with, or someone who you went to high school with. If you know the person and are able to contact them directly, write the company down.
- The last five companies you're going to obtain from www.Indeed.com. Indeed.com is a job-posting site that compiles job listings from almost every job-listing site on the Internet. You don't need to go to Monster.com and CareerBuilder.com. All the listings on these sites are aggregated and listed on Indeed.com. Now search for open positions based on your qualifications and restrictions. For instance, if you're a student majoring in finance and want to live in the NYC area only, you will search "finance degree, New York City" and see what openings come up. Find five open positions that interest you and write the companies and positions down.

Table 5–1 is an example of what your Excel document should look like (company and contact names are only examples).

TABLE 5–1. Initial Target List

Company	Contact	Open Position	Action
Selected Companies			
Pepsi			
Google			
Apple			
JPMorgan			
Amazon			
Know Someone			
CitiGroup	Adam Smith		
John Deere	Julie Williams		
AT&T	Jim Moore		
NYPD	Tim Harris		
State Department	Susan Richards		
Indeed.com			
Marsh & McLennan		Risk Analyst	
NY Life		Marketing Associate	
NBCUniversal		Ad Sales	
Nielsen		Analyst	
Fidelity		Financial Advisor	

Now you've got a starting point; you've triangulated your position and have a map to orient your attack! Also remember that these companies and names are not written in stone. Feel free to add or move around companies as you progress and continue to network with the people in your community. This is just a starting point.

STEP 2: IDENTIFY OPEN POSITIONS THAT YOU ARE INTERESTED IN

The next step is to visit the website for each of the corporations that you have listed and search for open positions that you are interested in and also qualify for. Most corporations have a "careers" section on their website that lists open opportunities. Identify these open positions and list them in your attack plan. If you cannot find any open positions that fit your interest or qualifications, then write down the specific division within the company that interests you, like Operations or Accounting.

TABLE 5–2. Target List with Open Positions Added

Company	Contact	Open Position	Action
Selected Companies			
Pepsi		New Product Marketing	
Google		Ad Sales	
Apple		Retail Store Salesperson	
JPMorgan		Equities Trader	
Amazon		HR Business Partner	
Know Someone			
CitiGroup	Adam Smith	University Recruiter	
John Deere	Julie Williams	Store Manager	
AT&T	Jim Moore	GNOC Operations	
NYPD	Tim Harris	Police Officer	
State Department	Susan Richards	Foreign Service Officer	
Indeed.com			
Marsh & McLennan		Risk Analyst	
NY Life		Marketing Associate	
NBCUniversal		Ad Sales	
Nielsen		Analyst	
Fidelity		Financial Advisor	

The reason why this step is important is because when you begin reaching out to veteran employees, you can't just tell them that you want to work at Google or JPMorgan. Remember what we discussed earlier: People like to help people who know how to help themselves. You have to give the people you're reaching out to some direction or a starting point from which they can determine how to help you.

At the end of this step, your attack plan should look like the example show in Table 5–2.

STEP 3: IDENTIFY AND REACH OUT TO VETERAN EMPLOYEES AT EACH CORPORATION

The third step is to identify and connect with veteran employees at each of the corporations. There are many different ways to do this.

Utilize Your Professional Contacts

Take a hard look at all the contacts in your personal and professional network. Does anyone work at any of these corporations? Do any of your contacts know a veteran who does and is able to make an introduction? Can your parents or any of your old high school friends introduce you to anyone?

Here is an example email you could send to one of your contacts. (Note: Mr. Stevens has been a friend of your father's for many years. He has a son named John who is a few years younger than you are. Mr. Stevens has also been a financial advisor for JPMorgan Chase for almost 20 years.)

Subj: Careers at JPMorgan

Hi Mr. Stevens,

How's your summer going? I hope you're enjoying the nice weather. How is John liking college?

I'm back from the Army and trying to figure out what to do next. I'm very interested in pursuing a career at JPMorgan and was hoping to be able to sit down with you and ask you some questions about your career path. Please let me know if you have some time within the next few weeks. Have a great week!

Respectfully,
Mike

Visit the Company's Website

Many corporations are developing Employee Resource Groups (ERGs) for employees who come from minority population groups, such as Latinos, African Americans, and now military veterans. The goal of the ERG is to help recruit, retain, and provide support for minority employees within the corporation. Many corporations highlight these groups and provide contact information for group leaders on their websites. Look online and see if the company you are interested in has a veteran ERG. If so, reach out to the contact; these groups exist to help you get into the company.

Here is a sample email that you could send to someone who you do not know but whose name and contact information is posted on the company's website.

Subj: U.S. Marine interested in a career at Amazon

Hi Karen,

My name is Mike Abrams and I'm a Marine and Afghanistan veteran. I obtained your contact information from the Amazon.com website.

   I'm very interested in pursuing a career at Amazon and was hoping to be able to speak with a former military employee for a few minutes to gain a better idea on whether I'd be a good fit for the company. My resume is attached and a short summary of my military experiences is listed beneath my signature as well. I am available to speak at your convenience. Thank you very much for your time!

Respectfully,
Mike Abrams

Look Up a Veteran Employee on LinkedIn

Sending someone who you don't know a message on LinkedIn.com is perfectly appropriate. Let's say, for example, that you are searching for a veteran who now works for PepsiCo. You can either search for "Army Pepsi" or click on the Pepsi company page and scroll through the employee profile pages for former military personnel. When you find one, write an email like the following sample.

Subj: Transitioning Soldier / Career at Pepsi

Hi Lisa,

Your profile came up in my LinkedIn search. I'm a transitioning soldier interested in pursuing a career at Pepsi. Would you have a few minutes to talk about how you got your start at Pepsi? Thank you for your time!

Respectfully,
Mike Abrams

Note: Only reach out to one person per company at a time. You don't want to message three or four different people at the same company because in many instances the veterans within the company talk regularly and "distribute" the recruiting duties or career inquiries among each other. Email or reach out to one person at a time. Give that person seven days to respond. If they don't respond, you can choose to reach out to them a second time or to engage another person. Remember that this takes time; you're not going to build a relationship over night. Be patient, but keep attacking!

At this point, your target list will look like the example shown in Table 5–3.

TABLE 5–3. Target List with Action Items Listed

Company	Contact	Open Position	Action
Selected Companies			
Pepsi	Lisa Atwater	New Product Marketing	Sent email (EM) 5/28
Google		Ad Sales	
Apple		Retail Store Salesperson	
JPMorgan	Paul Stevens	Equities Trader	Meeting 6/3 at 10a
Amazon	Karen Mills	HR Business Partner	Call 6/5 at 2p
Know Someone			
CitiGroup	Adam Smith	University Recruiter	Follow-up (F/U) next week
John Deere	Julie Williams	Store Manager	EM 5/28
AT&T	Jim Moore	GNOC Operations	
NYPD	Tim Harris	Police Officer	EM 5/28
State Department	Susan Richards	Foreign Service Officer	Connecting me to a veteran
Indeed.com			
Marsh & McLennan	Dan Baskin	Risk Analyst	EM 5/28
NY Life		Marketing Associate	
NBCUniversal	Janet Cruz	Ad Sales	Spoke on phone, F/U 6/5
Nielsen		Analyst	
Fidelity	Amanda Smith	Financial Advisor	EM 5/28

STEP 4: SECURE A JOB!

Don't get frustrated! You're not going to get hired overnight. The people who you're reaching out to have full-time jobs, families, and a million other things going on. It may take several days for them to get back to you. But when they do, be prepared to adjust your schedule to meet their availability. You want to make it extremely easy for them to help you.

The following is a sample email response. It's short, to the point, and provides all the information the person needs to get an understanding of who you are, what you want to do, and where you'd make a good fit in the company. You're helping them help you!

RE: Subj: Transitioning Soldier / Career at Pepsi

Hi Lisa,

Thank you for the quick response! I'm available next Mon, Tues, and Wed any time before noon. My cell is 555-201-9876. Please let me know what's convenient for you. My resume is attached for your review and I also applied online for the following position:

Job ID: 7394267 - New Product Marketing Associate
Applicant ID: 112398

Looking forward to speaking with you and have a great weekend!

Respectfully,
Mike Abrams

SUMMARY

Applying for jobs and internships is a daunting task. You can't just shoot from the hip and expect the best. Having a basic attack plan to organize your thoughts, opportunities, and contacts will help you ultimately be successful in your pursuits. The outline recommended to you in this step is just a starting point. Feel free to alter and change it based on your personal preferences and circumstances. The key is to have a plan, adapt it as you move forward, and keep attacking!

VETERAN PROFILE

Courtesy of Val Nicholas

NAME: Val Nicholas

TITLE: Vice President, Business Development, NBC News
National Co-Leader, NBCUniversal Veterans Network

BIO: Val served in the United States Army as a 31M, multichannel communications specialist running the communications center for the 11th armored cavalry regiment. He is now the Vice President of Business Development at NBC News; he leads the development of new ideas for NBC News to grow its brand.

WHAT IS NBCUNIVERSAL?

NBCUniversal is one of the world's leading media and entertainment companies in the development, production, and marketing of entertainment, news, and information to a global audience. NBCUniversal owns and operates a valuable portfolio of news and entertainment television networks, a premier motion picture company, significant television production operations, a leading television station group, and world-renowned theme parks. Comcast Corporation owns a controlling 51% interest in NBCUniversal, with GE holding a 49% stake.

WHAT IS THE NBCUNIVERSAL VETERANS NETWORK?

The NBCUniversal Veterans Network was first established in July 2010, launching with employee-based chapters in both New York and Los Angeles.

In 2011, a chapter was launched in Miami. The company-wide affinity group was modeled after the successful veteran's organization that was previously created at Universal Studios Orlando, which at the time of launch was an NBCUniversal joint venture. Currently, Universal Studios Orlando is also a part of the NBCUniversal Veterans Network. The Veterans Network has more than 720 members nationally, 200-plus members from within NBCUniversal and 450-plus members at Universal Studios Orlando.

The NBCUniversal Veterans Network mission statement is to foster a business culture that recognizes, supports, develops, and promotes the unique characteristics of veterans and active military throughout NBCUniversal.

WHAT DOES THE NBCUNIVERSAL VETERANS NETWORK DO FOR VETS?

We help recruit and support veteran employees by reaching out to different non-profit partners to connect veterans and their families to NBCUniversal employees. In addition, once a veteran employee has been hired, the Veterans Network serves as a base of support for that member in several ways, including a mentoring program (if the veteran so chooses to enroll) and events focused on growing the professional and personal development of veterans and their allies.

The NBCUniversal Veterans Network is proud to be a central part of the team that originated the "Got Your 6" campaign that launched on May 10, 2012. Nearly every major studio, broadcast, and cable network, talent agency, and guild in the entertainment industry united with top-tier non-profit organizations to launch the Got Your 6 campaign, which will create a wide array of opportunities for veterans to successfully convert their leadership and operational training into positive civilian roles in communities nationwide.

In addition, the NBCUniversal Veterans Network is a supporter of and has volunteered with numerous organizations, including Operation Gratitude, Wounded Warriors, USA Cares, the Vet Hunters Project, and the USO. The NBCUniversal Veterans Network continues to build ties to the military and veteran communities.

HOW CAN VETS LEARN MORE ABOUT THE NBCUNIVERSAL VETERANS NETWORK?

As of right now, veterans can find out about career opportunities and contact the company through the web at www.nbcunicareers.com.

Courtesy of Shutterstock.com

WHEN NETWORKING DOESN'T COME EASILY

The more you network, the more you will come into contact with different types of person-alities and varying styles of networking. Two people can approach a room full of people from completely different perspectives and achieve the same results. One can work the room in a gregarious manner, meeting many different people and engaging in multiple con-versations, while another can be quieter and engage in fewer, more engrossing conversa-tions. However, when they walk out of the meeting, they both have found new contacts, made new friends, and secured referrals and leads. The differences in their approaches to networking are a result of their personality traits. The first person, the gregarious one, is more of an extrovert, and extroverts get their energy from being around and interacting with people. The second person is more of an introvert, and introverts gather their energy inter-nally. In this step, we discuss how introverts can also be great networkers.

THE INTROVERT'S NETWORKING ADVANTAGE

Many introverts, like the one we described, are good networkers. They know how to use their introverted nature to their advantage. They are often good listeners. They notice details and remember important facts, and because introverts often let others do more talking, the other person walks away thinking the introvert was a brilliant conversationalist. It's sort of like the old saying, "It's better to be thought a fool than to speak and remove all doubt." We know from research and experience that when one person has done the majority of the listening, people who have observed the conversation as well as the speaker believe the listener is the more intelligent of the two.

Introverts are also more thoughtful and frequently the first to give compliments, to remember special events, and, of course, to remember to say thank you. Remember Step 4, in which we discussed the characteristics of great networkers? Three of these characteristics are common in introverts—**Bearing, Tact,** and **Unselfishness**. If you are, or suspect you are, an introvert, the first step is to understand and appreciate your best qualities and to learn how to use them to your advantage in networking.

THOUGHTFUL LISTENING

Listening carefully to others is a skill most extroverts need to work on. It comes easier to introverts, who naturally absorb and use what they hear. Introverts generally spend more time listening and less time talking. Did you ever have a battalion commander who knew your name and knew where you were from? How did it make you feel when he called you by name and remembered that you were a big Giants fan? Now compare that to when another one of your commanders called you only by your rank because he didn't know you. It makes a big difference to know that someone cared enough to remember something about you, even if it's just your name and where you're from.

Most people are in one of two states during a conversation: speaking or waiting to speak. Waiting to speak is a bad listening habit. If you are waiting to speak, it means you are thinking about what you want to say, which means you are not listening. Introverts can take advantage of their listening skills to build sound relationships, which is at the heart of being a good networker. There are some listening behaviors that are important for you to be aware of so you can avoid them in your practice to become a good listener.

Good listeners engage in active emphatic listening. Normal American conversational speech is about 25 to 50 words per minute. Normal comprehension, on the

---

POOR LISTENING BEHAVIORS

- Focusing on the other speaker rather than what he or she is actually saying
- Ignoring or shutting out what you don't understand or don't like
- Letting your emotions bias or filter what the other person is saying
- Daydreaming or letting external environmental factors interrupt your concentration
- Interrupting before the speaker is finished

---

other hand, can occur at 400 to 500 words per minute. In other words, you are capable of listening at a rate eight to 10 times faster than the other person is capable of speaking. This is nothing to celebrate. It's the reason for the most common bad listening habit—daydreaming. When you listen to someone speaking at a speed that's only about a tenth of your listening capability, your mind tends to fill its leftover capacity with other things.

These other things can then crowd out the conversation, and you lose some of what's being said. The cure for this inevitable tendency of the mind to wander during conversation is a discipline called active listening. Active listening is a way of giving your mind jobs to do that are concerned with the conversation. These jobs keep it focused.

TECHNIQUES FOR BETTER LISTENING

The following are three techniques that you may want to consider as skill builders for better listening.

First Listening Technique—Playing Back

One of the most powerful listening strategies is the technique of playing back. Listen to what the other person says and play it back. This is particularly useful in a networking situation for introverts because it helps you check your interpretation of what the other person has said, and it actually makes the other person feel good. Beyond that, however, it is effective because it forces you to think and process what the other person says. You don't want to simply repeat back the other person's own words (although you may want to do that periodically in small bits to check that you understand the person). To keep the conversation moving, you need to deal with the meaning of what the other person says. Playing back has the additional benefit of opening the other person up. Everyone has a desire to be understood, and playing back what the person has said almost invariably encourages the other person to provide additional information.

Second Listening Technique—Summarizing

Summarizing is like playing back, except that it happens less frequently, and it involves more than one thought. As you process what the other person is saying, fit it together into a theme or concept so you can summarize a list of points the person has made. Like playing back, this technique has benefits at two different levels: First, it lets you check your understanding, and second, it forces you to attend to what the other person is saying so that you can create the summary later.

At various points in the conversation, use a lead-in phrase and then list the points the other person has made: "If I have heard you correctly, you believe . . ." Summarizing shows the other person that you are listening, and that's an important part of building the relationship.

Third Listening Technique—Reflecting Emotion

Reflecting is a form of playing back, but it applies to emotions rather than facts. Whenever you hear a sign of emotion in the other person's conversation, you may want to acknowledge it. This shows the other person that you are attending to him or her as a person, and it builds your relationship.

Here are some examples of good lead-in phrases for reflecting emotion:

- "It sounds like . . . you're angry about the way that turned out."
- "I get the sense . . . you're going to take the offer."
- "I looks like . . . you couldn't be happier."

BE PASSIONATE

While many introverts don't relish the idea of walking up to a stranger and starting a conversation, discussing a topic that you are passionate about can make your shyness "magically" disappear. When you can focus on an aspect of business, industry, or a product or service you are especially passionate about, you will naturally speak with enthusiasm and conviction. Andrea recalls a conversation with an account executive, named Richard, who told her he became so nervous before meeting with a prospective client that he felt nauseous. Yet as soon as he started talking about his product, the benefits of which he truly believed in, he felt comfortable and at ease. It helps when introverts have a focus and a genuine reason to make a contact.

ELEVEN NETWORKING TECHNIQUES FOR THE QUIET NETWORKER

Under certain circumstances, most of us do feel shy, reticent, or introverted, regardless of what label you put on it. Half of us feel shy all the time, and the other half part of the time.

We've all felt stuck in the doorway of an event, thinking, "Should I walk into that crowded room or go back to my hotel room (or dorm room or back home)?" Yet we know that a key component of successful networking is visibility. You can't get that visibility in a hotel room, dorm room, or your bedroom, unless you are networking over the Internet (more on that later in this chapter).

Networking is all about making connections, building relationships, and developing advocates—people who know us, what we do, and what we are capable of doing so that they can become our marketers. Here are eleven tips on how to successfully network even when you are feeling shy.

1: Have an Objective

Be truthful with yourself. Too much self-improvement advice begins with "goal setting" only and no progress is ever achieved because goals are long term and have no quantitative measurements. Instead, set objectives, which are short-term, goal-oriented, measurable, and meaningful. Set goals for opportunities you have to expand or to nurture your network, and then set achievable measurable objectives that can be counted.

- When attending a networking event, set an objective to meet and follow up with at least two people. By "follow up," we mean that within a week you have sent an email or made a telephone call.
- At the next sit-down event you attend, set an objective to sit next to someone new. Think of three questions you can ask to learn about his or her background and interests.
- Once a week, go through your contact list or LinkedIn connections list, and set an objective to select four to six individuals to email or call. The contacts should be individuals who you have not heard from recently. Use the opportunity to "check in" to say hello and ask how they are doing.

- Set an objective to once a month have breakfast or lunch with a friend, colleague, or associate, particularly someone you have not seen for a while.

2: Take Baby Steps

The concept of networking, or building your network, can seem to be a daunting goal when you look at the "big picture." However, when you break a project down into smaller pieces (objectives), you can approach it bit by bit. You can only win the war one battle at a time. Think of the wisdom from the ancient Chinese proverb, "The journey of a thousand miles begins with a single step."

Writing this book was a huge undertaking for us. We had to break it down into baby steps—research, outline, take notes, draft one chapter at a time, proofread, and edit. We had to break it all down into manageable and measurable pieces. Rome wasn't built in a day!

Standing in the doorway, a networking event can seem scary. Take it step by step. Start by smiling. When you enter a room, whether you are aware of it or not, you are being observed and judged. People make what scientists call "microevaluations," or what laypersons call "snap judgments." Human beings have done this for hundreds of thousands of years; this part of our evolutionary development allowed our species to first survive (fight or flight complex) and then evolve with both our animal brain and eventually our cognitive or thinking brain. It is part of who we are and what we are, so please, no moral judgments of whether it is fair, just accept the practice. In less than a second, people will form what amounts to a full profile of you. They will create a lasting (sometimes lifelong) impression of your intelligence, world view, likability, and a wide range of other characteristics. By the way, you do the same thing. We all do it.

It is up to you to make this initial microevaluation image as strong and as positive as possible, and you can do this with an opening smile—the strongest, most positive nonverbal message known to human beings. If you don't smile, the initial impression will almost always be neutral to negative, and you've started with an unnecessary hill to climb. Make it as easy on yourself as possible—SMILE!

Establishing eye contact with people in the room will give you a greater chance of making a positive impression. Eyes can be the door to a conversation. You can tell if someone is receptive to a conversation just by glancing into his or her eyes. We can't explain the analytical and clinical reasons behind this phenomenon here, but try looking into the other person's eyes and you will soon find it works. You must experience it, and you will recognize the person's level of receptiveness when you see it.

When you meet someone, whether you just go up and introduce yourself, some-one introduces him or herself, or a third party makes the introduction, repeat the name of the person you have just met. This will help you remember their name. Next, to get the conversation going, you can ask what is known as an "open-ended question."

As previously discussed, an open-ended question is one for which the response cannot likely be a short one- or two-word answer (definitely not a "yes" or "no" question). Socrates was a master at this kind of question. He would ask questions of people because he truly was interested in assisting them. Open-ended questions help us to surrender control of the moment. Open-ended questions are not asked just to give the other person a choice of responses, but instead, they really allow the person to tell us what is going on in his or her mind.

CHARACTERISTICS OF OPEN-ENDED QUESTIONS

- Surrender control of the conversation (or confirm the other person's control)
- Tend to be lead to longer responses, which provide more information about the other person's interests and feelings
- Often include answers involving emotions that you can use to practice feedback

3: Begin with a Compliment

This is a wonderful way to start a conversation. Everyone loves to be complimented on something. Find something sincere to compliment people on any time you have an opening to start a conversation. By smiling and adding their name to the compli-ment you double the chances of making a great first impression.

4: Use a Script

If calling back to follow up on a new contact makes you a bit nervous, develop a short yet detailed script to use. Write the key points and rehearse the script until it comes across naturally. Besides your script, have notes to refer to about the person you are calling. After you do this a few times, it may become second nature to you and you may be able to get by with just your notes. Using a script is a good way to develop confidence.

5: Work on Making Eye Contact

Not making eye contact with someone you have just met is a huge mistake and can be disastrous. Not only does it give the impression that you are not listening or paying attention, but the person with whom you are speaking may consider you rude. Even worse, avoiding eye contact can be interpreted as body language that you have something to hide.

Making eye contact shows people that you are confident, trustworthy, and respectful. It's not a staring contest by any means, but being able to look someone in the eye and give your undivided attention goes a very, very long way.

6: Attend Events and Then More Events

You can only learn by doing. Just reading this book alone will not make you a better networker. You have to get out and attend events where there are people to meet. Naturally, you will be inclined to start in your own friendly territory and attend those social functions. This approach is okay for a start and okay to continue as a regular practice, but you need to spread your wings and attend many other functions. Many civic, social, fraternal, political, and special interest groups hold local events and many host regional and national functions where you can network. Sources include the local Chamber of Commerce, the Better Business Bureau, community development groups, business development and economic development organizations, veterans clubs, sales and marketing clubs, speaker clubs, and the list goes on and on.

The local papers list these events as well as the websites of the various organizations. Many groups sponsor breakfast, lunch, and dinner meetings as well as cocktail receptions and other social events where people gather for the express purpose of networking. Trade associations and professional societies hold many meetings as part of their service-based agendas. By Googling any profession, skill trade, or special interest and the word "association" or "society," you can find lists of the organizations that represent and support the interests of that group. Most have websites, blogs, tweets, and other special media sites that describe the organization and a calendar of events that they sponsor.

Your goal is to find these events and attend. Veterans who attend and network these events will have a distinct advantage over their peers who do not. The reason is simple. The business decision makers, the employers, the thought leaders, the deal makers, and the movers and shakers attend these events, and the veterans who meet and network with these influential people will be remembered when opportunities arise.

7: Attend Events with a Purpose

Instead of just going to meetings and events for the general purpose of networking, attend only those events where you have a specific purpose in mind.

A friend of Andrea told her that he once attended an industry event for the sole purpose of meeting the speaker. The speaker was a prominent leader in the field, and Andrea's friend was writing a book related to this field and wanted to be able to send it to the speaker for an endorsement when it was finished. Therefore, the friend's objective at this event was to introduce himself to the speaker and establish a reason for a follow-up contact. He didn't care about anything else at this meeting. If he met others, that was a bonus, if the food was good, that was a bonus too. But neither interested him. His objective was clear, and he accomplished it.

8: Set Up One-on-One Meetings

Next time you go to a networking event (or to any event), make it a networking opportunity. Give yourself an objective to connect with just one person and set up a follow-up, one-on-one meeting. Have this meeting at a comfortable place and at a time when you both can relax and get to know one another.

Coffee shops are good venues; no one will rush you, and many have comfortable seating arrangements conducive to conversations. It is much easier to get to know someone in this atmosphere than at events and other get-togethers.

9: Do Your Networking at Your Highest Energy Level Time of Day

We all have a time of day when we feel more energized, when our circadian rhythms peak. If possible, set up meetings, make phone calls, attend events, and even write your follow-up emails and thank-you notes during these high-energy times. This may not be possible if you have to attend an evening meeting and you are a morning person, but you can still deal with it. Pace yourself during the day (or even take a quick "power nap") to conserve your energy for later when you need it. The important thing is to know your own cycle and prepare ahead of time.

10: Set a Time Limit

One "quiet networker" Andrea knows gave this advice on dealing with networking events. She sets a time limit, and says to herself, "I'll go to the meeting for one hour and then I will go back and relax." She feels she can successfully gather her energy for an hour, whereas a full evening would be overwhelming. By using this strategy (small baby steps), she gets herself to the meetings knowing its "only for an hour." Use this tactic in making calls. Decide how much time you will give to the task, and stick to it. Don't be unrealistic; start small and remember to take baby steps. When you achieve your objective, you will be energized to continue on for longer the next time.

11. Recharge and Reward Yourself

Plan a schedule so you have time to recharge and reward yourself. This is particularly important for college students who may be working full or part time and going to school. You are not invincible, and you need to recharge your batteries from time to time. Do something nice for yourself. Reward yourself for accomplishing each objective and for each "baby step" along the way. You deserve a reward, even if it is as small as reaching around and patting yourself on the back.

NETWORKING ON THE INTERNET

Online social networking is an efficient way to establish and maintain relationships with others in your field. Finding and meeting people who can help you with contacts that can then be helpful in job searches, sales leads, and other business contacts is easy to do with the help of the Internet. Introverts may be particularly attracted to networking online because it may seem more comfortable. While there are many advantages of using online tools to assist your networking, the one major disadvantage— and it's a big one—is that it isn't face-to-face contact (even if you are using video conferencing). Face-to-face, eye-to-eye contact is the only way we know of to build true reciprocity with another human being. The theory of reciprocity simply states that if you do something for someone they will generally feel obligated to return the good will. This is the reason proper networking is so successful.

Digital networks are weaker links, but they do extend a person's reach further, even across industry and geographic boundaries, which helps people link up by skill level and talent needs. Supporting networking online also encourages the spread of new ideas at a very rapid pace. The best characteristic of digital social networks is that they are completely inclusive, unlike some of the more traditional face-to-face organizations. Digital networks welcome anyone. However, this benefit is also a weakness.

Too many people use social networking sites in a ubiquitous, incessant, compulsive drive to make dozens to hundreds of digital connections that lack true meaning. Real networking has a foundation in face-to-face encounters. Digital social networking should be viewed as a support and supplement to face-to-face networking. The daily (and sometimes hourly or more frequent) check-ins and shout-outs are a form of social contact different from networking and thus should be viewed and treated differently. There is no question that some people gain some traditional networking benefits from the micro-contact approach, but the personal ties are not that firm and if they are not reinforced by face-to-face encounters, there will be no real long-term trust or reciprocity established.

For better or worse, the traditional face-to-face networking encountered through smaller membership-based, agenda-based organizations generally creates stronger networks because most members know each other, and thus favors and sharing of information are encouraged and will certainly be returned. Digital networks, in contrast, create a much less loyal connection and therefore are not likely to create the environment for as many favors.

People build trusting relationships with others they know by looking them in the eye, shaking their hand, and getting that "intuitive feeling" about them. As fast and efficient as the Internet is, it doesn't facilitate trust building. There is still no known substitute for face-to-face contact. Despite the time, distance, and technological advantages of online networking, this downside has yet to be overcome. You cannot build rapport and trust online. This chemistry is still done eye to eye in the physical presence of another person.

While we encourage the use of technological tools, they are still just tools to support what you must do primarily in person. There is a chapter in this book especially devoted to social media.

SUMMARY

Sun Tzu wrote in his book, *The Art of War,* that if you know your enemies and know yourself, you will not be imperiled in a hundred battles. This step is about knowing yourself so you can minimize your weaknesses and take advantage of your strengths in order to benefit the most from networking opportunities. Don't ever try to be someone who you're not. Be yourself, know your strengths and limitations, and do the best you can with the hand that you were dealt.

VETERAN PROFILE

NAME:	Johnathon Lang
TITLE:	CUNY Hunter Student and NBCUniversal Client Partnership Development Intern
SERVICE:	United States Army, Iraq Veteran

Courtesy of Johnathon Lang

I enlisted in the U.S. Army, at the age of 18, in February of 2004. While in Iraq, I spent the majority of my time away from the large forward operating bases, instead working out of a small combat outpost in a northern suburb of Baghdad. Our daily missions varied greatly: One day I was tasked with helping out on a medical mission at a local school, the next day providing security for an Islamic religious procession, another day sharing lively meals with a large group of neighborhood elders as they tried to reach consensus with my superior officers on issues affecting their communities. My hardest days saw my comrades and me in active combat engagement with insurgents.

Upon returning home, I was faced with a new adventure: transitioning out of the military while continuing on to live a life of purpose. I had seen some of my closest friends die in Iraq; they were strong, motivated, and smart until the day they passed away. If they had made it home with me, I am sure that they would have continued on to do even greater things than what we accomplished together in Iraq. That left me, now 21 years old, with this question: How do I live on to honor my friend's lives?

Coming from a family of blue-collar workers and local entrepreneurs who saw little need for higher education, I learned from a young age to have a negative perception of attending college. In the military, I got a chance to work with outstanding people from many different walks of life, including quite a few college grads. These college grads more often than not were military officers, U.S. government civilians, or private contractors. Their attitudes about life, their socioeconomic trajectories, and their ability to make an impact on the world were generally appealing to me; therefore I decided that I would use my GI Bill benefits to find out what college was about when I got home.

After starting classes at Lehigh Carbon Community College, I quickly came to find that my professors encouraged me to think outside of the box, valued the military experiences that I brought to classroom discussions, and took an active interest in my personal, professional, and intellectual growth. I especially enjoyed my Spanish and Cultural Geography classes. I continued on for two years, taking classes full time at LCCC from Monday to Thursday and working with an Adventure Challenge Therapy program for at-risk youth from Friday to Sunday.

Eventually, I transferred to CUNY Hunter and enrolled in a professional development program for veterans, called Four Block, which provides resources, training, and networking opportunities to student veterans as they navigate the respective civilian-sector fields that they are interested in.

The experience working with Four Block greatly expanded my perspective on what various businesses do, how to make myself more valuable to them, and how to help them better understand what I can offer. My professional networking skills especially improved while I was working with Four Block. Previous to participating in the program, I had a negative perception of the word "networking." Networking wasn't a word the people I grew up around used; we made friends, not "networks," or so I thought. Furthermore, in my experience as a soldier in a line combat unit, it was nearly out of the question to approach a senior officer or NCO on a personal level. We were there to do our jobs as soldiers, not to schmooze and kiss the backsides of higher-ups. However, with all of the exposure that Four Block gave me to different ideas and companies, I quickly came to realize that networking really is just another way of saying "creating relationships."

For as long as I could remember, if a situation arose where I could use my knowledge or relationships to help a friend of mine, I would do so. Likewise, I wouldn't hesitate to reach out to a friend who might be able to aid me in solving a problem or reaching a goal. Professional networking is essentially just a fancy name for people on the higher end of the educational spectrum doing the same thing. As I realized this, things began to work out well for me at the networking events that Four Block put on with its corporate partners. In large part because of one of the relationships I forged at NBCUniversal's networking event, I eventually got the chance to participate in an internship at the Spanish language television network Telemundo. This has proven to be a fantastic experience for me, allowing me to work in a medium that I am passionate about, while at the same time allowing me to collaborate with great people who are helping me to further improve my professional skill set. It really is all about relationships.

Courtesy of Shutterstock.com

EXPAND, ORGANIZE, AND KEEP YOUR NETWORK GROWING

Imagine if you only cleaned your weapon and ensured it was functioning properly right before you engaged the enemy. Sounds ridiculous, right? In Iraq and Afghanistan, we were constantly cleaning our weapons due to the sand and grit. There is no worse feeling than having your weapon jam during a firefight. Think of maintaining your professional network the same way. If you're not consistently keeping in touch with your contacts and developing new relationships, then the opportunities available to you will jam up. In this step, we will give you tips on how to organize and follow up with the people who are already in your network (that's right, you already have a network, remember?) and establish a system that works for you to help you continue to grow and nurture each relationship that you make.

ORGANIZING AND KEEPING TRACK OF YOUR NETWORK

Don't expect this section to be full of high-tech jargon and recommendations for state-of-the-art computer hardware and software. Our theory is that you should keep it as simple and convenient as possible. You can use index cards, LinkedIn, or a program like Microsoft Excel or Outlook. Whatever system you decide to use, from Post-it notes to the latest computerized database system, it needs to be easy to use and simple to access or you will not use it consistently. Your system should work for you; you should not have to work for your system. The master networkers live by this axiom. The information they need is always at hand because their system is organized and accessible. Take time to set up a system, and then make sure to keep it up to date.

SETTING UP A NETWORKING DATABASE

- First enter contact information: name, title, company/school, address, phone number (cell, land line), fax number, email address, URL if appropriate, website, Facebook page, blog sites, Twitter address, and other social media addresses
- Enter each contact's preferred method of communication
- Enter "details" you want to remember such as branch of the military service, personal interests, books they like, clubs they have joined, sports they enjoy or play, food they like, their majors in school, their hobbies and interests, arts and entertainment interests, music and bands they like, family information, organizations to which they belong, their job information, and birthday and holiday information.
- A, B, C Prioritizing
- History of contacts and conversations
- Best time and place to contact

No matter how you choose to organize your database of network contacts and information, the important thing is to have a system and to stick to it. A key to successful networking is follow-up. Having a well-organized and up-to-date database, and a system to access it, will help you do this.

FIND OUT THE BEST WAY TO STAY IN TOUCH

When you meet someone you want to stay in contact with, one of the things you will want to ask is, "What is the best way for us to keep in touch?" Everyone has a preferred way to communicate. Don't assume that because your peers use text and email that these are the automatic preferred methods. Some people still prefer the telephone or face-to-face meetings.

Even if a person can't take a call, voice mail may work for them. For these people, a series of voice-mail messages may be perfectly suitable. Other people prefer email and are good at responding quickly, as you should be. Many younger people respond primarily by text and not by phone. Whatever the preference, you need to know so that your communications are as efficient as possible. This kind of information should be recorded in your contact database.

NOTE IMPORTANT DATES, BIRTHDAYS, AND ANNIVERSARIES

Find out the dates of birthdays, anniversaries, and other important occasions of your network contacts. Knowing such details provides an opportunity to get in touch with a card, email, text, or phone call.

Andrea always asks about birthdays—not necessarily the year (that could be problematic), but the month and day. This information is recorded in her contact database. Then each month she sends out an appropriate birthday greeting, cards for some, emails and phone calls for others. The fact that you remember is the important thing. Anniversaries, birthdays, and special dates are opportunities for you to reconnect and be in touch. Be alert to what people mention about these dates. Some people are proud of certain anniversaries, and the fact that you remembered will help grow the relationship.

Mike always reaches out to his veteran buddies around November 10, the Marine Corps Birthday.

FAMILY, INTERESTS, AND HOBBIES

Ask your network contacts about their families, interests, and hobbies. This kind of information gives you conversation starters (everyone loves to talk about themselves). It also provides you with information that helps you to stay in touch. Finally, this kind of information can provide you with ideas that can make you a resource for the person and turn you into a strong contact for him or her.

WAYS TO KEEP IN TOUCH AND SHOW APPRECIATION

Once you are armed with information, here are some ways you can use it to keep in touch and help build your relationships.

Handwritten Notes

We know the art of handwriting notes, especially for younger adults, is sadly disappearing. The U.S. Postal Service reports that only 4% of mail is personal correspondence. However, this mode of communication is a powerful key to success. What makes certain companies, organizations, individuals, and even branches of the government stand out? Differentiation is the way to stand out and get noticed. If you send handwritten notes, we guarantee they will be noticed and read. Think about it. When you open your mailbox, doesn't a handwritten envelope stand out among all the other mail, and don't you read it first, even before your email? And doesn't the thought cross your mind, "Someone is thinking of me"? A personal note is the most effective way to connect and reconnect with others and make them feel good about knowing you.

Thank-You Notes

One of the very best and least expensive public relations tools you can use is the simple thank-you note. You can never say "thank you" too many times as long as it is sincere.

EIGHT GOOD REASONS TO SEND HANDWRITTEN THANK-YOU NOTES

1. For time and consideration given to you.
2. For being interviewed for a job.
3. For a compliment you have received.
4. For a piece of advice you have received.
5. For business you have received.
6. For a referral you have been given.
7. For a gift someone has given you.
8. For help someone has given you.

It makes good sense to have note cards and stamps close by so that when you have some "found time" you can write a note or two and drop them in the mail.

Now there is software online that can produce a note card with your personal message in a handwriting font; thus, the note appears handwritten even though you have typed it on your computer. The difference is you simply print it, put a stamp on it, and mail it through the postal system. Check Andrea's website (www.selfmarketing.com) for more information on this service, which she uses.

Other Notes

Besides the thank-you note, there are several other types of notes that you can send any time to stay in touch and be helpful.

- **FYI (for your information).** You can send articles, clippings, or URL addresses that may be of interest to people in your network. These notes can be related to the recipient's business, former branch of the military, college courses, family, hobbies, personal interests, or something you think they might be interested in. Include a brief note, such as, "I thought of you when I came across this and thought you might (enjoy it, find it useful, be interested in it, want it for your files, etc.).

- **Congratulations.** Send one of these notes for a new job, a promotion, an award, an honor, or any event for which your network contact received recognition. This is a perfect opportunity to stay in touch.

- **Nice talking with you.** Andrea and Michael send these notes after a phone conversation (especially a phone appointment or conference call), a meeting, a chance encounter and conversation, and always after meeting someone new at an event.

- **Thinking of you.** These notes are sent for no particular reason other than to stay in touch. They are easy to use, as you can buy a card with this sentiment and just add a brief note.

"THE POWER OF THREE" NOTE PLAN

You may be thinking, "This is a lot of notes and cards!" and "Who has the time for that?" Here is a technique Andrea adopted and has used successfully for years. It is easy and does not take much time from your busy day. Moreover, we can say from experience that it will be sure to pay off in building solid networking relationships.

Every day, send three handwritten notes. Make them short notes that express any of the messages we have discussed. Some of the people you can send these notes to include:

- Fellow veterans
- Fellow students
- Former co-workers
- Friends
- Family members
- Club and association members
- Former teachers
- Prospective contacts
- Customers

If you write and send just three notes a day, by the end of the workweek you will have contacted 15 people, and by the end of the year, 750 people (assuming you take a couple of weeks off). Try to do these handwritten notes in addition to the thank-you and follow-up notes you would normally send.

Writing these notes should not take more than 10 minutes a day. You can write them either first thing in the morning before work or classes, during lunch, during your commute (by train or bus), or after your day ends, whenever works best for your schedule. Writing notes is easy once you get in the habit. Your note does not have to be perfectly crafted; it is the thought that counts.

TAKE FULL ADVANTAGE OF EMAIL

The handwritten note is a special note. However, in today's world we are fortunate to have a way to be in instant contact with many people all around the world. In fact, there is very little excuse for not showing appreciation or following up in a timely fashion with email. It is perfectly appropriate to send a thank-you note for any of the eight reasons mentioned earlier via email. It is also fine to send an article of interest as an email attachment.

Be careful to not bombard your network contacts with articles, notes, or (shudder) chain letters that are making the rounds on the Internet. Remember, you are extending a professional courtesy, and the message should be tailored to the recipient, not be a mass mailing. Make sure you have a valid reason to send the information, and always include a personal note. We will talk about networking etiquette in the next chapter, but for now remember to follow one fast rule about email correspondence: Always reply to emails within 48 hours of receipt. Not responding quickly makes you appear uninterested and even rude.

SEND GIFTS TO SHOW YOUR APPRECIATION

Sometimes it is appropriate to show appreciation with a gift. Sending a gift sets you apart—it differentiates you. When is it appropriate to send a gift? Send a gift after completing a project, when someone gets promoted, for a birthday or holiday, or when someone has done you a special favor. In business and academic situations, you need to be careful about the nature of the gift. Keep in mind, this is a gesture of appreciation and you do not want to place the recipient in the awkward position of having to turn down your gift due to a company or school policy.

In general, food is the best kind of gift in this situation. Most businesses or universities that do not allow gifts to employees and professors will allow a gift of food that can be shared with all. Some good choices include a fruit basket, a popcorn tin, or a box of candy or other edible goodies.

FOLLOW-UP: THE KEY TO KEEPING YOUR NETWORK ALIVE AND GROWING

You could be the master of working a room and leave each networking event with a pocketful of business cards, but if you do not follow up with these people and others already in your network, you will never be successful at networking. Follow-up is key.

When Should You Follow Up?

There are four absolute "must" follow-up situations. When you follow up in these situations and in the prescribed time suggested, you will be successful at creating and maintaining an active list of contacts who trust and respect you and who will gladly help you out when you find the need to ask. Here are the situations and how to follow up:

Four Absolute Must Follow-up Situations

1. Within 24 hours of a meeting, send a note, email, or call to say any of the following, depending upon the circumstances of your meeting:
   - "How nice to meet you."
   - "Thank you for your time and consideration."

- "We should meet again."
- "Thank you for the useful information."

This is not only a courtesy, but it will also differentiate you from the myriad others they may have met.

2. If you have promised to send materials, to phone to set up a meeting, or to pass on a referral, keep your word and do it within the time promised or sooner. It is easy to make these promises at a meeting or event, but it is the person who follows up in a timely manner who is remembered and trusted.

3. Call within two weeks after having made a suggestion to get together, whether over a meal or at a more formal meeting. Just saying, "Let's do lunch" is not an effective networking technique. Don't suggest it unless you mean it; then follow up to set a specific date and place. Twenty-four hours before your get together, call again to confirm. When you follow up in this manner, you will be perceived as being sincere and professional.

4. If a contact gives you a referral or passes on your resume to help you out, be sure to thank your contact and let him or her know the results. You should also do this for any tangible advice given to you from a network contact. People who offer help to you in any form deserve to know the results of their advice. More importantly, they absolutely deserve a thank you.

Following up not only shows good communication skills but also builds solid relationships for the future and shows respect for others. It helps people remember you and makes them more willing to want to continue helping you.

BECOME A RESOURCE FOR OTHERS

Share your skills and experience, happy in the knowledge that you are helping friends and fellow students and colleagues. Other people appreciate and seek out knowledgeable individuals who give generously of their expertise. When you have been a resource to others, people are more willing to help you when you ask.

FACE-TO-FACE TIME

When you can spend time with someone in person, it is always more powerful, effective, and memorable than carrying on a conversation by phone, text, or email. The reason for this is what we call "chemistry." Sociologists call it "rapport," but many people just refer to it as "connecting."

You know the feeling—the energy and excitement you feel when you have made a strong bond with someone over common interests or issues. This rapport can only be made and felt when you are in the other person's physical presence and can look into their eyes. The bond of rapport can lead to a colleague, a friendship, and certainly a strong network contact.

People love doing things for and with other people they know and like. The presence of this positive phenomenon has positive health benefits. Making network contacts actually helps strengthen a positive mental outlook for people.

In today's busy world, it is increasingly difficult to find the time to plan to make face-to-face contacts. Distance is also a mitigating limiting factor. However, like many other things, if you make a plan, you are much more likely to carry out the activity. Make a plan to spend some face-to-face time with your network contacts. Because face-to-face meetings require more planning, schedule them at least 30 to 60 days in advance.

You have to be both persistent and creative to make sure you get this face time. In addition to traditional meetings such as breakfast, lunch, dinner, and after-work outings, suggest meeting for coffee, tennis, or golf, or meet at a museum or industry or academic meeting. Think creatively. Everybody is busy, and people will appreciate new and unique suggestions. Be persistent. Face-to-face meetings are invaluable in building solid networking relationships.

PLAN HOW TO KEEP IN TOUCH WITH EVERYONE IN YOUR GROWING NETWORK

As your network continues to grow, you will want to have a system to stay in touch with each of your network contacts. We are frequently asked how we keep in touch with the several thousand people on each of our networking lists. Here is a way to do it.

Use A, B, and C Categories

Divide the list into three categories: A, B, and C. The "C" list is made up of "touch base with" people. These are casual acquaintances, interesting people we have met and with whom we would like to stay in touch, and with whom there is no immediate personal involvement or business connection. Each C category person gets a quarterly contact of some sort. Holiday cards are appropriate.

The "B" list is made up of "associates." These people are people with whom we are actively involved, either professionally or personally. We find ways to meet each of these individuals in person, for a meal, coffee, tea, snack, or a chat at least two times a year. In addition, we send them up to six personal notes a year. Also, they should get called every other month just to say hello. These individuals get holiday cards and gifts too.

The "A" list is made up of "close friends and associates," and we try to see these individuals in person at least four times a year. They should get special gifts and often we contact them with personal notes and calls. These are the people who should receive individual articles of interest as well as newsletters and holiday cards.

The A, B, and C lists are not static, and these rules are not forged in stone, but this system represents a plan and provides a road map for how to manage a contact list effectively.

SUMMARY

When we were overseas, we didn't know when we were going to be attacked. The enemy didn't send us an email saying, "We're going to attack your FOB from the northwest at 0800 on Monday." But we were always ready for it. We cleaned our weapons, ensured our gear was working properly, and remained ready to go at all times. In the civilian world, your professional network is now your primary weapon. You must continue to clean, provide maintenance, and ensure you have a network that's ready to provide you assistance and opportunities when you need it. If you only contact people when you need something from them you won't get much help from anyone. Remember what we keep saying throughout the book: If you help others, you'll eventually have a squad of people at the ready to help you.

VETERAN PROFILE

Courtesy of Peter J. F. Meijer

NAME: Peter Meijer

TITLE: Director, Student Veterans of America

BIO: Peter enlisted in the U.S. Army in 2008. While a student at Columbia University, Peter deployed to Iraq as an embedded combat advisor with the Iraqi Army. Through Operations Iraqi Freedom and New Dawn, Peter participated in bilateral missions with brigade, division, and command-level Iraqi Army units across United States Divisions Central and South. Peter is a 2012 graduate of Columbia and a member of the Board of Directors of both Student Veterans of America and the Cape Eleuthera Foundation. In addition to work with SVA, Peter consults for independent films on issues facing the veterans' community and continues to serve as a non-commissioned officer in the U.S. Army Reserves.

Student Veterans of America is a nationwide non-profit service organization dedicated to providing military veterans with the resources, support, and advocacy needed to succeed in higher education. Since our inception in 2008, SVA has organized over 500 student veteran chapters in all 50 states. For maximum impact, our chapters are centered on a peer-support model to provide student veterans with a sense of purpose. SVA chapters have been organized at all types of institutions of higher education, from two-year community colleges to four-year public and private universities.

SVA is recognized by the Joint Chiefs of Staff Warrior and Family Support Office as an innovative example for others to follow, and by Secretary Eric K. Shinseki of the Department of Veterans Affairs as the "premier advocate for veterans seeking better jobs and better futures through education."

WHAT DOES SVA DO FOR VETERANS?
Chapter Support

In 2007, student veteran groups at schools from Michigan to California and Texas to New York realized they were all facing the same issues in adjusting to the academic environment. Instead of trying to reinvent the wheel, these individual groups came together to found Student Veterans of America. Today, SVA provides support to over 500 campus-based student veteran chapters nationwide, advocating for national veterans' issues and delivering resources to enable student veterans to achieve their educational and career goals.

Each SVA chapter is run by student veterans for student veterans. Our peer-support model provides a renewed sense of community for returning servicemen and women by utilizing a template that has been linked to improved academic performance and higher overall well-being. SVA chapters are the "boots on the ground" that foster a robust, cohesive community to help veterans matriculate through college. While social interactions and group initiatives provide the foundation for individual success, the chapter's actions as a whole can influence the entire campus community. Advocacy efforts, for example, highlight veterans' issues for administrators and have led to improved policies. Raising awareness can reduce military stereotypes and create more respectful classroom environments. Long-term initiatives reinforce the unity of the group and restore a sense of purpose for veterans to achieve their full potential, overcome transition challenges, and graduate with a market-valued degree.

National Leadership Institute and National Conference

At SVA, our strength lies in our ability to band together as a team. Toward that end, through annual meetings at our National Leadership Institute, National Conference, and regional events we seek to build student veterans' organizational capacity and give student veterans from across the nation a chance to network with other student veterans and established leaders at the local, regional, and national levels. SVA works with the Bill and Melinda Gates Foundation, the U.S. Chamber of Commerce, and the Chairman of the Joint Chiefs of Staff Warrior and Family Support Office to host our events and give student veterans the opportunity to expand their skills as leaders in their local communities.

Scholarships/Internship Support

SVA offers scholarships to supplement student veterans' earned educational benefits, but even though education is our focus, our work does not end at graduation. Through partnerships with national employers such as Google, JPMorgan Chase, and CitiBank we offer career counseling and job fairs to set student veterans on a path for success. Student veterans with dependents may not be able to take the unpaid internships needed to become competitive in their chosen fields. For them, we work with employers to provide stipends and access to paid internships in several career fields so student veterans have access to every advantage of their civilian peers.

How Can Vets Get Involved with SVA?

Anyone who is interested can visit SVA's website at http://www.student veterans.org to learn more. While we have worked hard to keep up with our rapid expansion, we are still only present at 10% of campuses across the United States. Student veterans attend over 6,000 educational institutions in the United States, from traditional brick-and-mortar universities to community colleges, technical schools, online institutions, and everywhere in between. Veterans on campuses with SVA chapters can join simply by following the instructions laid out on our website. We ask for no dues and have no membership requirements other than that a group be recognized by their school as a student organization and that the chapter's first two point of contacts be student veterans. We are also always looking for veterans to get involved with mentorship programs post-graduation.

For student veterans on campuses without SVA chapters, we encourage you to create a student veteran group at your school and apply for membership. In the military we function best as a team, pairing strengths to accomplish our assigned mission. Our uniform may change when we swap rucksacks for backpacks, but our ability to accomplish whatever task lies ahead remains an integral part of who we are as veterans. Student Veterans of America: yesterday's warriors, today's scholars, tomorrow's leaders.

Courtesy of Shutterstock.com

NETWORKING ETIQUETTE

Etiquette is just plain good manners and common courtesy. Successful business relationships, just like successful personal relationships, rely on this. In this chapter, we will take a look at some rules of etiquette that relate to networking activities and should also be remembered and observed in any business or social situation.

GENERAL RULES FOR NETWORKING EVENTS, MEETINGS, OR OTHER EVENTS

1. Arrive on time, or better yet arrive 10 minutes early. Showing up late is disrespectful and is a red flag of poor character or time management. It signals you think your time is more important and valuable than those at the meeting. Early arrival demonstrates enthusiasm and respect for people's time. Furthermore, an early arrival gives you time to settle in and further plan your activities.

2. Place you name tag on the right side and as high as appropriate on your garment. This puts it in a direct line of eye contact with people you will meet and helps people see and remember your name.

3. Exchange business cards with ease. Place several loose cards in your right pocket or in a spot where you can reach them easily without digging or rummaging through your pockets, purse, or wallet. Make sure your business cards are fresh and up to date.

4. Do not walk around with a stack of resumes, and do not just hand out your resumes to everyone you meet. Keep your resume in a folder or attaché until it becomes obvious it is needed.

5. Make eye contact with each person you are about to meet. Looking someone in the eye shows respect and that you are honest and trustworthy.

6. Shake hands (if appropriate) firmly. There is nothing worse than a cold, fishy loose grip. On the other hand, do not use a death grip either. This is not a contest to prove your strength. There are different types of handshakes that signal via body language your intent. A handshake that puts one person's hand firmly and purposefully on top of the other person's hand is a signal of dominance and power.

   Grasping another person's arm or shoulder while shaking hands signals that you have supreme confidence and are someone who assumes command of the situation.

7. Be aware of the difference between business, social, and personal space. Business space is five or more feet apart and conveys proper business distance. Social space is between two and four feet apart and conveys a warmer, friendlier feeling amenable to discussion. Personal space is closer than two feet and causes many people discomfort unless they invite you into their space with a double-grasp handshake, pull you in, place a hand on your shoulder, or otherwise move to close the space.

8. Welcome others into your conversation with grace and a smile. Extend your hand(s) with the palm up, welcome them, and be inclusive.

9. Don't try to eat and carry on a conversation. Do one or the other, not both at the same time.

10. If you drink and carry on a conversation, either use little or no ice or wrap napkins around the glass. A cold glass leads to a cold handshake.

GENERAL RULES FOR MEALS AT LARGE EVENTS OR PRIVATE FUNCTIONS

1. Turn off your cell phone and beeper. Answering—or worse yet, making—a call at such an event shows disrespect. It says the people at the event are not important.

2. First introduce yourself to the persons seated on your right and then your left. Then introduce yourself to the rest of the table. As others join the table, introduce yourself and others to them.

3. Wait for those at the head table to begin eating, or if at a private meal, wait for the host or hostess to begin. If you are the host or hostess, you must begin.

4. Allow your guest to order first. Direct the server first to your guest, then you. Then select your entrée accordingly. It is safest to pick something in the mid-price range.

5. If you don't know which utensil to use, working from the outside in is always a safe start. Alternatively, watch the host or hostess.

6. Keep your napkin on your lap until you leave the event. If you leave the table, temporarily place the napkin on your chair. Once you have finished your meal, place the napkin next to your plate.

7. Water glasses and salad plates work this way: Liquids on the right, solids on the left.

8. When you are finished, place your knife and fork in a parallel position across the center of your plate.

9. Even if you are still hungry, stop eating if everyone else at the table is done.

10. Don't talk with your mouth full.

11. Hold off talking about business until the main course is cleared. This allows ample time for small talk and getting acquainted. In addition, the servers will be out of the way.

12. Ask before you take notes. It is perfectly acceptable to take notes at a business networking event, but first ask out of courtesy. Use a small notepad or index cards, not a full-sized notebook or a laptop.

MAKING INTRODUCTIONS

In the business world, when introducing two people, defer to position and age. Gender is not a factor. Try to include something that the individuals might have in common. An introduction is normally made in this logical order:

1. **Older to younger.** For example: "Mr. Walters, I would like to introduce you to my daughter Sue, the president of her eighth-grade class."

2. **Professional colleague to professional colleague.** For example: "John, I've been meaning to introduce you to a former co-worker of mine, Linda Jones. She and I worked together at Ace Tomato Company."

3. **Senior executive to junior executive.** For example: "Susan, I'd like to introduce you to our logistics manager, Joan Roberts. Joan, please meet our CEO Susan White, who I believe got her start in business in logistics."

4. **Fellow executive to client.** For example: "Robert, I would like to introduce you to the Purchasing Manager of XYZ Company, Joe Smith."

5. **Personal contact to business contact.** For example: "Maria is a friend of mine, and I wanted her to meet someone who knows as much about accounting as she does. Maria, this is Don."

EMAIL AND IM ETIQUETTE

Email and instant messaging/text messaging make our lives easier. They are immediate, efficient, and convenient. They are wonderful communication tools; however, sometimes your messages can be misunderstood if you do not follow certain conventions. We realize young people have a unique language and relaxed rules for spelling and grammar online. However, keep this fact in mind: **Digital messages don't disappear.**

Any digital message or signal that you send stays in cyberspace forever. You can delete messages from your computer, but once sent, they can still be recalled. Once you hit the send button, the message is no longer yours. It belongs to whoever has possession of it. Also bear in mind that email and IM lack the vocal inflections and body language required to express tone, regardless of the icons, tags, and other devices that attempt to convey emotions and feelings. You can't digitize body language, yet. Here are some digital communications etiquette tips:

1. Keep digital communications brief, to the point, and focused.
2. Use meaningful, thoughtful subject lines.
3. Use a format: purpose, body, and action.
4. If you need to send a long document, send it as an attachment.
5. Do not forward jokes, chain letters, flame letters, or other junk email or other IMs.
6. Never email or IM when you are angry or emotional, or when your judgment is clouded. Better to wait a few hours or a day.
7. Always re-read your message before hitting send. *Make sure you are saying what you want to say.*
8. Answer all emails within 48 hours.

PHONE ETIQUETTE

1. Return all phone calls within 48 hours, even if you don't have an answer yet. Let your caller know you are working on the issue.
2. When making a phone call, ask the person if it is a good time to talk; if not, ask when a good time is, and follow the other person's lead.
3. State the purpose of your call and indicate that you would like a few minutes of the person's time. Don't take any longer unless the other person insists.
4. When you answer, try "This is _____, how can I be of assistance?" or "How can I help?" This approach saves both the caller and you time, and saving a minute or two on every phone call can add up to a big block of saved time every day.
5. When leaving a message, clearly and succinctly state your name, the purpose of the call, and the action you need. Most importantly, when leaving your number, speak slowly and clearly.
6. When calling a contact referral, state your name and who referred you. For example, "Hello, my name is Mike Abrams. Andrea Nierenberg suggested I give you a call to ask if you would be kind enough to tell me about how you have been so successful in launching a new product during this recession. Is this a good time to talk?"
7. Smile when you are talking. The other person can't see you, but he or she can tell by your voice whether or not you are smiling.
8. Don't multitask while on the phone. People can tell when you are trying to do several things at once. It is rude and disrespectful.
9. Don't put the other person on speakerphone unless it is absolutely unavoidable or the person requests it.

THE RIGHT WAY TO ASK FOR A FAVOR

When you have been a good resource to others, it is easy to ask for a favor. Most people are happy to help, especially if you know how to ask. Here are some opening lines you can use:

- "Perhaps you could help me . . ."
- "Who do you know that . . .?"
- "Would you feel comfortable referring me to _____?"
- "I would really appreciate your help with . . ."
- "I'd like to get your advice on . . ."
- "Maybe you could steer me in the right direction."

- "If you were in my shoes, what would you do?"
- "How would you handle this?"
- "There is something that I could really use your expert advice on."
- "It would be wonderful if I could get your opinion (or advice) on something. Would you consider helping me?"

Always remember to say thank you and follow up with an email, handwritten thank-you note, and a gift, if appropriate.

FOLLOWING UP

Following up is always good networking etiquette.

1. Always send a thank-you note or an email within 48 hours after a meeting. Thank your contact for his or her time and consideration, and confirm any follow-up steps.
2. Get permission for any "next steps." Ask when would be a good time to call or get together. Also ask, "What is the best way for us to keep in touch?" The person may prefer IM, email, telephone, letters, or a face-to-face meeting. These steps show respect for the other person's time and preference.
3. Be sure to follow up when asked specific questions. When asked specifically for a referral, materials, data, your resume, or other source material or information, ask, "When do you need this?" And then send it on time—or earlier.

NETWORKING AT A NON-NETWORKING EVENT

Networking, if you think of it as connecting, learning about and helping others, and building relationships, can be done anywhere at any time. The purpose of a networking meeting is to share personal information and ask for referrals. The purpose of a wedding reception, or a dinner, party, or many other social events is to celebrate. Does this mean you should not try to meet people and begin to establish relationships at such functions? Of course it doesn't. However, the proper way to do this at social events and other non-networking events is with discretion. Follow these rules and you won't get into trouble:

1. Recognize where you are, the purpose of the event, and why you are there.

2. When you come across a potential network contact, graciously suggest that perhaps this is not the best time to discuss business/networking opportunities and suggest a call for a later date. Offer some options. This is a perfect example of why you need business cards.
3. Ask permission before exchanging business cards or personal information. Then the exchange should be as discreet as handing a tip to a maître d'.
4. Recognize that there are several types of establishments, such as private clubs, where conducting business is simply not allowed. Be aware of where you are and follow the prescribed behavior.

KEEPING SCORE

For some people, networking means that they do someone a favor and a favor is owed to them in return. It is almost as if they keep a scorecard for every contact. We just believe in helping others, and if we receive something in return, we consider it a gift, not a right or a privilege. Here are some guidelines on "keeping score":

1. Always return a favor given to you.
2. Don't expect or demand that a favor be returned to you.
3. Give only for the sake of giving.
4. Under promise and over deliver.

NETWORKING COMPETITION

We would like to make another point about competition and networking. Some people by their nature are very competitive. While there is nothing inherently wrong with "keeping score" and trying to be the best networker possible, you need to be cautious about turning your networking into a competition just to win or to build up the largest number of contacts, or to be the first in your graduating class to get a job or a promotion using networking. Networking is a professional experience. Using it to keep pace with your classmates or to rack up numbers of contacts, or solely as a means to an end, is a misuse of networking's purpose.

SUMMARY

This step stresses the importance of etiquette in networking. It is important to recognize that networking and good manners are compatible. Networking is about building relationships with others, and as in any relationship, common sense and courtesy are musts.

VETERAN PROFILE

NAME: Stephen Clark

TITLE: Acting Director, CUNY Office of Veterans' Affairs

Courtesy of Stephen Clark

BIO: Stephen Clark is the University Interim Director for Veterans Affairs at the City University of New York. He is a member of the New York City Community Advisory Board for the U.S. Army and serves as its Education Subcommittee Chairperson; is recognized as a Center of Influence by the U.S. Army 1st Recruiting Brigade; is the Vice President of the New York State Advisory Council for Military Educators; and is a member of the National Association Veterans Program Administrators Education Committee. Mr. Clark earned a Bachelor of Arts in Liberal Arts and Sciences and a Master of Arts in U.S. History at the City College of New York. He is the son of a U.S. Army veteran.

WHAT IS THE CITY UNIVERSITY OF NEW YORK?

The City University of New York (CUNY), comprised of 24 institutions, is the nation's leading urban public university. Realizing that thousands of men and women from the metropolitan NYC area served the nation in Operation Iraqi Freedom, Operation Enduring Freedom, and other military initiatives around the globe, senior university administrators recognized an advancing need to develop programs and services for soon-to-be returning military personnel and responded by establishing the CUNY Office of Veterans' Affairs (COVA) in the spring of 2007.

WHAT DOES THE CUNY OFFICE OF VETERANS AFFAIRS DO FOR VETS?

COVA, located within the CUNY Division of Student Affairs, has a dedicated mission of welcoming and supporting veterans, reservists, survivors, and their family members in recognition of the contribution they make as citizens and students, and fosters their success in college by assisting in their transition from military to student life. To that end, COVA designed, coordinated, and networked critical support programs and services, and cultivated public and private partnerships to further develop a sense of community with faculty, staff, students, and the administration throughout the university.

Projecting that CUNY may collectively enroll one of the largest veteran populations in the country, the university allocated funding to establish campus-based programs and initiatives, resulting in on-campus space being allotted for student veterans to meet, study, and socialize. In addition, campus staff included into their professional portfolio veterans' affairs, and on many campuses staff were added to work entirely in the area of veterans' affairs, thereby establishing campus liaisons. As campuses developed their physical and staffing capacity to work with veterans, COVA further concentrated on outreach and recruitment in cooperation with the university offices of Enrollment Management and Admissions.

COVA recognized that the enhanced post–9/11 GI Bill enacted on August 1, 2009 would be an incentive for veterans to pursue a college education or to return to college after a leave. Collaborating with subject matter experts within veteran-oriented federal, state, and local groups, and in cooperation with like-minded community-based organizations, COVA leveraged its expertise and networking capability to deliver campus service centers focused on providing assistance in the areas of career, child care, disability, financial aid, and wellness and counseling. This resulted in student veteran success, measured by successful transition into campus life, retention, and degree completion. CUNY also funded the Project for Return and Opportunity in Veterans Education (PROVE) in 2007 as a partnership to augment the work of COVA, an initiative that began at the Hunter College Graduate School of Social Work, placing social work graduate students at a variety of CUNY campuses to support and facilitate student veterans' reintegration into campus and civilian life by assisting in the development of veterans clubs, associations, and social activities. PROVE became a recognized model of excellence; it was aided by continued university support, receiving an ACE-Walmart grant in 2010, and grant funding from the NYC Robin Hood Foundation in 2012.

Programs, services and initiatives for student veterans are critical components for any institution of higher education to provide. We owe student veterans a special debt in return for their service, and it is repaid in the currency of preparation and exposure to internships and workforce readiness, beginning with resume writing skills that enable veterans to translate their military experience into civilian language, providing job interview training, and helping student veterans understand that there are myriad career opportunities within corporations that are seeking the exact capabilities veterans possess as a function of their military service. It has been our experience at CUNY and COVA that to successfully facilitate the transition from campus to career requires us to utilize our personal networks, building upon our professional capabilities to empower student veterans' futures in civilian culture, and the way to do so is to lead by example.

HOW CAN VETS LEARN MORE ABOUT GOING TO SCHOOL AT CUNY?

To learn more about how the CUNY Office of Veterans' Affairs can help you, visit www.cuny.edu/about/resources/veterans.html.

Courtesy of Shutterstock.com

SOCIAL MEDIA: A FOCUS ON STRATEGY TO SUPPORT YOUR PERSONAL NETWORKING

Social media is a phenomenon where private interactive communication and mass collaboration techniques successfully combine, allowing individuals who are bound by a shared interest or purpose to transparently and collaboratively connect. If you think this sounds a lot like what many people already refer to as "personal networking" you are accurate. Long before social media, the Internet, wireless communications, instant messaging, email, and even before the telephone, successful people understood the power of social reciprocity and the building and maintenance of one's personal contacts for the benefit of both parties. In this step, we discuss how veterans can use social media to enhance their networking opportunities in order to make a successful military transition.

Social media is the online environment created for the purpose of instant interactive communication and mass collaboration. It is the old campfire, the 19th-century family dinner table, the weekly fraternal organization meeting, the PTA, the Sunday afternoon church social, the neighbors gathering at the backyard fence, and the social networking discussed in this book all rolled into one and magnified by some exponentially large number.

What makes social media different from anything man has done up to this point is the fundamental change in the form of human communication. We can now instantly communicate with one other person or millions of people in seconds through a variety of mediums using words, pictures, graphics, or code.

Literally any way digital content can be communicated to others is within our abilities. Social media, in this context, is about communities of individuals who have come together, joined by a variety of digital communication channels, (e.g., Facebook, Pinterest, YouTube, wireless devices, LinkedIn, Twitter, Digg, Meet-Up, Google+, personal blogs, etc.) and bound by a shared interest or purpose. This is what makes social media different from anything man has done up to this point.

The value of social media to support personal networking is found in the productive collaboration of multiple communities, on a massive scale, simultaneously and productively leveraging the knowledge, experience, background, thought leadership, intuition, research, and ideas of many people on a variety of issues, problems, opportunities, and solutions. The benefits of the diversity of heterogeneous thinking, (the wisdom of the crowd) all add to the value of a vast network expanding the value chain of individuals.

THE FUNCTIONING OF THE PARTS IS DETERMINED BY THE NATURE OF SOCIAL MEDIA

The gestalt or behavior of social media is determined by the purposeful configuration and functioning of the individual elements (1) strategy, (2) technology, and (3) audience. These three components are so unified as a whole entity that social media cannot be effectively described nor can it achieve its complete purpose simply by attempting to make the parts operate independently.

Social media is a phenomenon where private interactive communication and mass collaboration techniques successfully combine. It is a set of digital and electronic communication software and various digital technologies allowing individuals to transparently and collaboratively connect, vote, decide, share, judge, evaluate, see, talk, and network with each other. Technologies such as *wikis, social networking, blogs, video posting, peer-to-peer sharing, hash tags, email, instant messaging, cloud storage, bookmarking, share this, threaded discussions, idea engines, answer market places, prediction markets, virtual second worlds,* and *avatars* are just the current usable and acceptable technologies.

These technologies are not critical in and of themselves. They are parts of the whole phenomenon of social media and have a use, but without the strategic purpose or mission of interactive communication and mass collaboration providing a strategic gestalt, they are just individual technological game pieces.

The audiences for social media, by the nature of their demographic and psychographic characteristics, seek to organize and apply the technologies and parts of social media into a gestalt phenomenon that reconnects individuals and rejects the previous sociological trends of our culture toward atomism and the collapse of community that Robert Putnam described in his 2000 classic book, *Bowling Alone.*

There are two major audiences for whom social media can provide far-reaching benefits: individuals and organizations. The first group, consisting of individuals, is the only audience that we address in this book. Individuals have the potential to use social media to dramatically expand into communities of interest and participate at any level, from being an observer to being an influencer or thought leader of such groups. In addition, individuals can use social media primarily to communicate with friends and associates and secondarily to self-brand and self-market.

The social media revolution is driven by the millennial generation, which comprises 30% of the world's population. In the U.S. there are over 81 million people of this generation; they are the hip young people born between 1977 and 1997 that the author Don Tapscot called the "first net" generation. This cohort has changed the rules of communication for the rest of us (Tapscot, 2007).

To this fastest growing influential segment of the population, there is no difference between business and personal communication, no significant difference between public and private communication, and no difference between communicating between two people or two million people. Communication to them is a transparent collaboration between those with a common or shared interest.

Regardless of how progressive and enticing this may seem there is still a need to be cautious of the seduction of social media and the temptation to try out all the new cool social media gimmicks, tactics, ideas, concepts, and technology.

There has to be a better reason to become social media literate. One aspect of social media that needs to be reinforced by awareness and skill training is the proven success of strategically applying it to personal networking and job hunting. A great deal of research has clearly demonstrated the benefits of personal networking (referred to previously in this book as the "informal" job hunting approach) as the most effective tool for job searching and career advancement available to individuals. Another temptation is to repeat the Internet error—to use the vast potential of the medium to oversell and then underperform—by trying to overwhelm as many people as possible with technological cleverness and cuteness and then littering the space with spam, junk offers, and other clutter.

The social media train has supposedly left the station and individuals may feel technologically backward if they haven't kept up. They may feel handicapped if they don't have hundreds of Facebook friends, or a Twitter site, or several Google+ circles. This is the same type of thinking as the "ready, aim, shoot" mentality of the early days of Internet marketing and needs to be rejected. We should have learned the lessons of the dot.com mistakes, but sometimes it helps to be reminded of what went wrong with the killer app of the "www."

Peter Drucker, one of the great business thought leaders of the 20th century and author of the very first book on the profession of management in 1954, proposed three questions that represent a classic inquiry into strategic thinking. His three questions were:

1. What is your business?
2. What will be your business?
3. What should be your business?

The questions were seductively subtle, and often individuals, including senior executives, were put off guard by their seemingly simplistic substance and missed the important issue Drucker was trying to get them to see. For any individual or firm thinking about employing social media effectively, it would be wise to rethink and paraphrase Drucker's three questions as follows:

1. What is your social media strategy?
2. What will be your social media strategy?
3. What should be your social media strategy?

It may seem like a blinding flash of the obvious, but you must approach the job search as you would a full-time job, dressing and thinking and acting like you are being paid to do this. Approaching the job search or a career enhancement as a full-time job means writing a strategic personal business plan with seven components:

1. Mission statement
2. Vision statement
3. Background and situation analysis

4. Strategic objectives and tactics including self-branding and positioning
5. Targeting potential opportunities that include industry and skill analysis and assessment
6. Reassessing job skills to current and future needs
7. Social media literacy

As one considers the strategy of social media to support a job search or career enhancement one very critical point must be front and center: There is an enormous amount of data out there that demonstrates employers are looking for *good people* who can adapt to change and meet the ever changing needs of business. Employers want skills and characteristics that for the most part are transferable from recent graduates with formal education to military veterans.

Job seekers must be adroit at demonstrating their ability to translate their personal skills, abilities, characteristics, and background experiences into the skills that employers need now and in the future.

A significant amount of research and writing has been done in this area. Dr. Faulkner is currently involved in conducting another major survey on how the supply side—the employers—view, perceive, and use networking. The early results of this research confirm the data from dozens of previous studies showing that employers want and need "good people" but generally have trouble finding them.

The formal methods of job searching—including digital postings, job fairs, posting resumes on employer websites, recruiters, classified ads, cattle calls, mass mailings of resumes and cover letters, and even what we teach in our educational system—are not working very well.

This is demonstrated in the literature. The data indicates that there is more likelihood of a successful job search if the informal methods of personal networking and direct application to the hiring manager are the major tools used by job candidates. Of course, this is not to say other tools should not be used; they should be, but as part of a job search repertory that is situational and conditional depending on each candidate and job search.

THE GESTALT OF SOCIAL MEDIA—THE PARTS OF IT

There are really three components to social media:

1. The technology
2. The audience
3. The strategic purpose (the most important to you)

There are hundreds of technological tools and they will come and go, so don't get too wrapped up in the individual pieces of the social media technology—they are only the bridge from your strategy to the audience you want to reach.

The audience is your goal or the "who do you want to reach." Just because the technology can connect you with thousands or even millions of people doesn't mean you need to or want to. The author Peggy Noonan wrote something very profound recently in referring to the ability of the president to reach millions of people by social media. She said, "Big microphone . . . No message."

To integrate social media into your job search requires that the strategy be carefully thought out. How do you want social media to support your job search?

Just a decade ago there was no social media, as we think of it today, and therefore there was no need for a social media strategy *per se*. However every individual has the responsibility regardless of the time period—be it pre–social media, pre-Internet, pre-technological revolution, today, or in the future—to spend time daily on visionary and strategic thinking about the future of his or her social media activities, in addition to the time spent on actual tactics and implementing the items of the social media menu.

Social media, like any other phenomenon, does not operate in a vacuum, and individuals seeking the advantage of personal networking need to think about and plan how social media and their goals will be affected as the social, economic, cultural, and business environment changes.

While virtually no one could have predicted the coming and extraordinary growth of social media—a risk phenomenon we call a "Black Swan"—there were early adapters. These were the individuals who recognized the potential value of the possibilities of social media and then the software, technology, mediums, and tools.

These adaptors began as early as possible to explore the individual growth and networking possibilities of social media and established practices, benchmarks, and disciplined personal networking management processes of the new media, gaining a huge first mover type advantage. They became the disciples, teachers, and digital natives.

There were valuable lessons that some individuals learned from the dot.com boom and bust about maintaining disciplined strategic plans in the midst of speculative runaway technology and individual expectations. The twenty-somethings who came of age with the Internet saw it as a toy and had no idea what a real strategic plan was, or how to target an audience for networking or how to build an interactive online relationship.

As Figure 9–1 shows, the Internet was clearly a channel that the business market was using, but the business advertising dollars did not flow to that channel in pro-

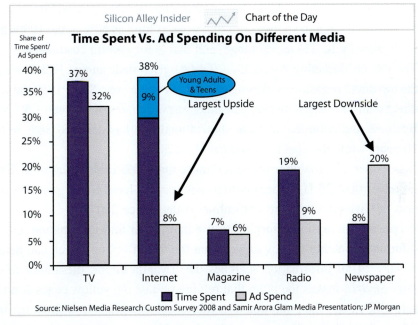

Courtesy of BusinessInsider.com

FIGURE 9–1 Time Spent vs. Advertising Expenditure on Different Media

portion to its apparent potential. As the graph shows, adults spend 29% of their time on the web, but advertisers are only putting 8% of their ad spending on the web. Meanwhile, newspapers only get 8% of our attention but 20% of the ad dollars!

The following are examples that demonstrate this thinking of individuals and consumers by their behavior.

THE OLD MEDIA CHANNELS

- According to the Federal Trade Commission (FTC), as of 2011 over 200,000,000 individuals have their names on various federal and state "Do Not Call" and "Do Not Fax" lists.
- According to the FTC, as of 2011 tens of thousands of consumers have their names on "Do not Mail" lists.
- According to the Direct Marketing Association, 44% of direct mail advertising is never opened.
- As a result of mismanagement, corruption, fraud, misuse, abuse, and the failure of firms to oversee commercial email, the 2003 Federal CAN-SPAN email law was passed. Once the killer application of the Internet, email marketing went

from the goose that laid the golden egg to the proverbial dead duck. Commercial email response rates that were as high as 60% in the 1990s are typically now in the 1% to 3% range, and that is for current customers.

- The Direct Marketing Association (DMA) gives their annual ECHO Award for the top direct response marketing campaigns of the year. Since 1980 the winning direct mail campaigns display consumer response rates of between 1.5% and 4%.

- Business and commercial trade show attendance has declined 38% in the last 10 years while the cost to attend has risen 50%.

- Newspaper advertising revenue fell more than 28% in one quarter in 2008 and no fewer than 20 U.S. metropolitan newspapers have either gone out of business or have gone to hybrid or online models since 2007.

- People are increasingly turning to the Internet to find information, even local information. Some figures suggest that the use of online search can be as high as 80% of all information searches. Dr. Lynella Grant, the author of *Yellow Page Smarts,* makes the point that relying on just the yellow pages is no longer safe. She makes the point that over half of all customers now go to the Internet first to find information, even for local products.

- The organization Generator Research predicts television advertising will fall by more than 75% in the next decade.

- Starting in 2007, radio advertising declined for 14 consecutive quarters.

- According to an industry expert, as much as 33% of all traditional advertising dollars are not only wasted, unproductive, and inefficient, but they cannot even be accounted for.

- 90% of the people with access to TiVo or other time-shifting technologies use them.

- Only 18% of traditional television advertising campaigns generate a positive return on investment.

- Only 14% of consumers trust advertisements, whereas 79% trust peer recommendations.

Over the years, consumers demonstrated time and again, with their buying behavior, that traditional forms of marketing, advertising, promotion, branding, sales, and even communication had low levels of effectiveness. Now, the appearance of social media marks a new form of communication centered around communities of similarly minded people abundant with passion, experience, thoughts, talents, ideas, solutions, and a desire to collaborate to improve their common interests. This is fertile ground for personal networking.

DATA ON SOCIAL MEDIA FOR THE GENERAL POPULATION

- There are over 700,000,000 Facebook users (over 300,000 are businesses).
- 200,000,000 people sign on monthly to Twitter and on average, spend 132 minutes.
- LinkedIn has 100,000,000 monthly visitors.
- According to the Pew Research Center, 95% of American adults with household incomes of $75,000 or more use the Internet regularly and own a cell phone. For American adults with incomes of less than $30,000, 57% use the Internet regularly and 75% have cell phones.
- In total, 73% of the American population uses the Internet regularly and two-thirds (65.8%) of adults with an Internet connection use social media in some form.
- 46% of the global population visits a social networking site daily; one-third of these visits (about 30% of the global population or 2.41 billion people) are looking for brands to interact with online.
- A recent Jupiter Research study found that 50% of Internet shoppers consulted a social media blog prior to making an Internet purchase. Furthermore there are more than 115 million active blog sites just in English, and perhaps twice that number if foreign language blogs are counted.
- A recent 2011 Pew Research Center survey on consumer access to news reported that between 2009 and 2011, the consumer audience fell for every channel of news media except online. It fell for cable 13%, for magazines 8.9%, for audio 6%, for newspapers 5%, for network news 3.4%, and for local TV 1.5%, whereas the online audience grew by 17.8%.
- In 2008, the most popular Facebook application was not a game, peer-to-peer music sharing, or a video or TV application. The most popular Facebook application was something called "Causes," with nearly 20,000,000 active monthly users. Causes lets users start and join causes they care about.
- By some estimates, the adoption of online voting in the future could save the U.S. economy an estimated $6.7 billion in lost productivity.
- A 2008 study found that over one-third (34%) of Americans turn to social media for health research and over half of the respondents (55%) said the most important reason to use social media over other online sites is to get a trusted cost for a procedure or medical equipment.
- According to a Nielsen 2010 study, U.S. Internet users spend three times more time on blogs and social media networks than email.
- 57% of American workers use social media for business purposes at least once a week.

- eMarketer projects that by 2012 more than 800 million mobile users worldwide will connect to social media sites using their mobile device, up from 82 million in 2008.
- The Library of Congress (LOC) has recognized the significance of social media and has established the National Digital Information Infrastructure and Preservation Program. According to its website the LOC is pursuing a strategy of collecting, preserving, and making available significant digital content, especially information that is created in digital format only. This work is being done so that current and future generations will have access to the content. In April of 2010 the LOC announced it would begin archiving all Twitter messages retroactive to 2006.
- According to the 2011 Pew Internet and American Life Project Study, two-thirds of adult Internet users (65%) now say they use a social networking site like MySpace, Facebook, or LinkedIn, up from 61% the year before. That's more than double the percentage that reported social networking site usage in 2008 (29%). And for the first time Pew Internet surveys show that half of all adults (50%) use social networking sites. The pace with which new users have flocked to social networking sites has been staggering; when first asked about social networking sites in February of 2005, just 8% of Internet users—or 5% of all adults—said they used them.

The media components of social media, (e.g., Facebook, Twitter, Google+, YouTube, Foursquare, BrightKite, Groupon, LinkedIn, etc.) and software and technological components, (e.g., blogs, digital video, bookmarking, microblogging, media sharing, aggregators, etc.) function to bring individuals, firms, and organizations together as collaborative communities working to solve problems, fill needs gaps, find solutions to problems, develop collective answers to questions, and provide the wisdom of crowds.

If Peter Drucker were alive today, he might ask this: What is your social media strategy?

Think about it—if you're an individual, don't you want to find a better, more efficient, more effective way to find, keep, update, locate, and communicate with friends, associates, family members, and persons of interest in communities of special interest? Through social media, you're able to:

- Gain more opportunities to build, develop, and improve your personal networking
- Get more personal branding and exposure for you and your ideas, beliefs, and values

- Increase online recommendations and referrals
- Get and give advice
- Share opinions
- Demonstrate your expertise
- Perform or publish your work
- Acknowledge something or someone
- Distribute software, content, or art forms (legally)
- Create targeted discussion groups
- Share photos, music, content
- Post and or get resumes
- Get answers to questions
- Play games alone or in combination with others
- Solve social, academic, political, scientific, geopolitical, engineering, and other problems
- Announce events and activities

Something that should be apparent to individuals is that social media requires a commitment to transparency, honesty, and open and authentic communication; this is a fundamental part of the theory of reciprocity, the foundation on which personal networking succeeds. The strategy imperative is to select technological tools that help achieve the purpose of networking. The whole purpose of social media (as was the whole purpose of the Internet, but we missed that one) is to create, build, and sustain relationships through communication channels that people prefer. Then, if appropriate, the relationship will turn into a long-term personal networking commitment.

Acquaintances will become close long-term friends. If building interpersonal, interactive sustainable relationships is the goal, then friendships, networking relationships, and long-term commitments will naturally result if that is appropriate. There are still some who say that despite the huge impact of the Internet, it did not alter traditional business as much as the hype predicted. These people will say that social media is similar—lots of hype, but when the dust settles we will be back to business as usual. The arguments that this thing called social media is mostly hype and will fade away are being countered by the successes of social media.

The debate on the exact impact of the Internet on our culture and business will not be resolved for many years to come. However, there is one critical factor, one variable, one externality that is in play today that was not as powerful a factor in the 1990s, and that is the generational demographics.

What force(s) have led us to this critical change at this point in time? The answer can be found in a combination of factors, such as the changing demographics of our population and the power of technology to produce ever more efficient and less cost-ly tools to communicate. We will see and experience the impact of a growing and younger work force dominated by people under the age of 30 that views communi-cation differently than boomers. To boomers communication is either private in nature and used only after business hours, or business in nature and used only dur-ing business hours. To the younger workers, there is no difference between private and business communication because almost all communications are or should be through social media channels, which means communication is cooperative and col-laborative in nature.

The population that has rapidly adopted the tools and technology of social media has a dramatically different perspective on communication. To them, communication (private or business) is 24/7 because they understand that the social media tools, tech-nology, and software have continued to be developed, improved, and deployed at ever more productive rates and efficient costs, helping to blur the lines and alter the para-digm of communication. Work and private lives can be blended because human beings are adapting to a form of communication, a form of cooperative leadership and work, that involves more collaboration teaming than a "here it is, this is the way it is going to be" approach.

The major factors in the rapid adoption of social media at this time are the grow-ing numbers of digital natives in groups of influence and power who believe per-sonal communication is not divided into personal and business, and the growing proliferation of social media communication platforms that are real-time and free.

The digital natives—the millennial generation—got it intuitively and hopefully more of us graybeards are coming to the realization of the benefits as well. To put it in terms we invented, the value is in the "workflow output measurement." Social media reduces inefficient and multiple individual redundancies but expands the real personal networking function. We will show this in actual cases in the final chapter, but it is simply accomplished by many, many people sharing experiences, reviews, complaints, ideas, and solutions and the output of these communities being produced with complete transparency.

BACK TO THE FUTURE

A side benefit of the growth in social media that not many people have spoken about is that all this reconnecting is hopefully rebuilding our social capital. In 2000, author Robert Putnum wrote the bestselling book *Bowling Alone,* in which he reported the results of his long-term study of the loss of social capital in America. Putnum traced the long, slow decline of group and social communities in America from the end of World War II to the late 19th century. His research demonstrated a decline in membership organizations of all types: from PTAs to trade associations; from bridge clubs to volunteer membership organizations; and from unions to bowling leagues. What concerned Putnam about the decline of membership organizations and groups was the resulting decline in social capital.

As Putnam pointed out, physical capital refers to properties of individuals and social capital refers to the connections among individuals—social networks and norms of reciprocity and trustworthiness that arise from them (Putnam, 2000). In Putnam's analysis we simply were no longer doing good things for others because of the subsequent decline in personal contacts with one another.

The term *social capital* itself was used by theoreticians, scholars, researchers, and others as early as 1916 to stress the importance of community involvement for successful schools. In the 1950s Canadian sociologists used the term to characterize the club memberships of well-to-do suburbanites.

In the 1960s urban specialist Jane Jacobs used the term to laud neighborliness in modern metropolitan areas. In the 1970s economist Glenn Loury used the term in his theory to analyze the legacy of slavery. In the 1980s the French social theorist Pierre Bourdieu used the term to describe the social and economic resources embodied in social networks. Putnam then added his insight that today's social media is connected to social capital, not just in the sense of individual social clout and companionship, but in terms of how both individuals (private good) and the community benefit (public good) (ibid, p. 20).

Now social media may be the catalyst that can reignite an awakening of social capital. While it may not be the face-to-face contacts that Putnam had hoped for, social media certainly encourages collaboration, teamwork, mutual obligations, and the norms of reciprocity (cooperation and work for the greater community good).

THE PERILS OF PREDICTIONS

Having positioned social media in this context, it is equally important to provide an abstract of contrary points of view, namely that some people believe we have already reached what they refer to as the "saturation level" for social media.

When anyone (even knowledgeable and respected sources such as Forrester) attempts to make predictions about anything in which "technology" is involved, one's first thought may be to wonder why would they want to expose themselves to eventual ridicule (people remember the bloopers, not who was right on target). By their nature predictions are risky gambits, which, at best, are similar to putting a puzzle together in the dark and without all the pieces, and then trying to describe the finished work in detail.

Social media is a phenomenon resulting more from changes in the forms of human communication than from insightful business managers looking for a better mouse trap. The principle or phenomenon and the technology are not the same thing; the technology is built based on the phenomenon. In practice, before a phenomenon can be used for technology, it must be harnessed and set up to work; phenomenon can rarely work in their raw form, yet today's predictions are being made using current technology.

SOCIAL MEDIA ISN'T FOR EVERYONE

Not every individual, business, or organization will adapt social media to their lives or business models. For some, as we will see, social media is not applicable, while others are just not ready to accept the benefits and value of social media. Misuse of social media can cause high failure rates. Social media is not suitable when deep analysis is required, when information is required from certain intermediaries or experts, when certain safeguards or security standards are required, or when sharing with large groups is inappropriate. Regardless, social media is a phenomenon that is having an extraordinary impact on individuals and businesses, and therefore should be understood, which is the purpose of this monograph.

A July 2009 Nielsen Study—the Global Online Consumer Survey—found that only 14% of consumers trust advertising, but 78% trust peer recommendations from social media. Furthermore, during the holidays, 81% of consumers will consult an online review prior to making their holiday purchase (Qualman, 2011).

There are other benefits related to the growth of social media with regard to transparency. For individuals the adoption of social media means we are composing and transmitting content in the forms of short messages, full text documents, video clips, and others by the hundreds or thousands destined to far-off places, thus extending our potential networks. The Gartner Group did an extensive study of social media beginning in 2009, and one of the most interesting findings is the striking discovery that most social media initiatives in companies and organizations fail. They either don't attract any interest or they never create any measurable business value (Ivey Business Journal, 2009).

What is surprising about this is that it appears most businesses and organizations are only reaching half of their markets on a channel that they have not even seriously considered. Additional strategic attention is necessary.

It seems many businesses and organizations either keep social media tightly corralled within existing marketing processes and operational procedures, or let it "do its own thing." Both approaches are wrong. Social media, whether it is based on a business model or for individual use, needs a strategic plan.

VETERAN PROFILE

Courtesy of Jason Hansman

NAME: Jason Hansman

TITLE: Membership Director, Iraq and Afghanistan Veterans of America

BIO: Jason enlisted in the U.S. Army Reserves in August of 2000 as a Civil Affairs Specialist. He was assigned to the 448th Civil Affairs Battalion at Fort Lewis, Washington and deployed to Mosul, Iraq as the Operations NCO for B Company, 448th Civil Affairs Battalion in 2004. He supported the 1st Brigade of the 25th Infantry Division for a 10-month deployment. He was honorably discharged from the Army Reserves in 2009 and now serves as the Membership Director for the Iraq and Afghanistan Veterans of America.

WHAT IS IAVA?

Iraq and Afghanistan Veterans of America (IAVA) is the first and largest non-profit, non-partisan organization for new veterans, with over 200,000 member veterans and supporters nationwide. IAVA is a 21st-century veterans' organization dedicated to standing with the 2.4 million veterans of Iraq and Afghanistan from their first day home through the rest of their lives. Founded in 2004 by an Iraq veteran, our mission is to improve the lives of Iraq and Afghanistan veterans and their families.

IAVA strives to build an empowered generation of veterans who provide sustainable leadership for our country and their local communities. We work toward this vision through programs in four key impact areas: supporting new veterans in Health, Education, Employment, and building a lasting Community for vets and their families (HEEC).

We create impact in these critical areas through assistance to vets and their families, raising awareness about issues facing our community and advocating for supportive policy from the federal to the local level.

WHAT DOES IAVA DO FOR VETS?

IAVA's programs empower and support our community both online and offline, expand our reach, and sustain our organization to make a deeper and lasting impact on veterans and their families for years to come. Our programs are scalable, flexible, and durable to make a positive influence on Iraq and Afghanistan veterans in an ever changing landscape of support and public awareness.

Health Programs
We know how hard going to, and coming back from, war can be. IAVA makes it a priority to ensure that both mental and physical health needs are being effectively addressed in our community.

- IAVA has connected more than 20,000 veterans with mental health support through our programs and referrals to best in class service providers. We recently announced a partnership with the Veterans Crisis Line to help our members in their toughest times of need. The partnership will provide a direct support line for IAVA members and our staff. And that means no waiting, no bureaucracy, and saving more lives.

- IAVA is also focused on the health of military families. Recently, IAVA helped spearhead passage of the Caregivers Act to help our nation's full-time caregivers for wounded veterans of Iraq and Afghanistan.

Education Support Programs

With hundreds of thousands of new veterans headed back to school under the new GI Bill, IAVA provides them the tools and support needed to make informed decisions.

- Over 560,000 veterans have already visited NewGIBill.org and used our innovative new GI Bill calculator to calculate their benefits and get one-on-one support from our new GI Bill experts on staff.
- IAVA has also partnered with companies like Veritas Prep to provide scholarships to our members for college test preparation courses to support them through every stage of the education process.

Employment Programs

No veteran should come home from Iraq or Afghanistan to an unemployment check. And to fight shockingly high jobless rates, IAVA has stepped up in a variety of ways through our Combat to Career initiative.

- This offers groundbreaking resources to our members, like providing 6,000 free business suits to veterans, helping hundreds of them navigate the job market at Smart Job Fairs, and providing critical training to vets through Google Resume Workshops.
- IAVA is also a force to be reckoned with on Capitol Hill. In 2011, when Washington was in a stalemate, we led the way to pass the Vow to Hire Heroes Act, our top legislative priority. This bill helped over 200,000 unemployed veterans during one of the worst economic situations in decades.

HOW CAN VETS GET INVOLVED WITH IAVA?

Vets who are interested in IAVA's programs can visit IAVA online at http://iava.org. This will give them information about all of our programs, as well as information about how to join the organization—membership is 100% free.

Courtesy of Shutterstock.com

TYING IT ALL TOGETHER

Now is the opportunity to choose, the decision time. As we said in the beginning of this book, nearly everyone has the opportunity to choose the pathway to his or her future: a pathway to success or mediocrity. Many people will never be aware that they have this opportunity and therefore will never choose consciously. The fortunate ones become aware of this opportunity and choose success; others are aware and choose not to put forth the effort. When you decided to serve your country during a time of war, you chose to put forth the effort.

Your military transition now puts you at another crossroads in your life. One pathway involves following along and basically handing over your future to whatever you believe life has to offer you, whether it is fate, randomness, luck, good decisions, or a combination of these and other things mostly out of your control.

The other pathway involves choosing networking as a life-altering technique and tool and then beginning—and never stopping—to use the technique and tool to choose your life options. Will you still face obstacles, setbacks, job losses, failure, defeat, uncertainty, randomness, and bad luck? Certainly. We all do. But your set-backs can be managed better and they should have a less detrimental impact on your life because you will have the safety net of your network. We cannot predict the future, but if you encounter any or all of these difficulties, you will have the tech-niques and tools to help you face them and realign yourself toward your new goals and objectives.

Many will want to make networking part of their lives; fewer will actually start, and more will drop away because of the commitment to hard work that's required. However, the dedicated ones will continue on and they will more than likely be suc-cessful in achieving their goals and objectives in life than others who choose to go with the flow.

Remember the foundational principles of your military transition that we dis-cussed at the beginning of this book:

- No one is going to give you a job.

In the corporate world, transitioning veterans are not that special. Although most employers respect and appreciate military service, it's not enough for them to pull the trigger and give you a job. You have to prove to them in some way that you will be a valuable employee.

- Win the high ground.

The "high ground" in your military transition consists of your family, friends, pro-fessionals, and veterans in your community. Build strong relationships with these people and you'll have the information and opportunities you need to figure out the next best step in your life and career.

- Find strength in service.

We are strongest when we are helping others. Focus on how you can continue to live a life of service and you will find your way.

Thank you for taking the time to learn and adapt some of these principles and techniques into your life. We would like to know how they work for you. Feel free to drop us a note, an email, or give us a call.

We wish you the best of luck in your military transition and beyond. Semper Fidelis.

VETERAN PROFILE

Courtesy of Marcia Shippey

NAME: Marcia Shippey

TITLE: Senior Manager, Property Tax Leader, Comcast Veterans Network (VetNet)

BIO: Marcia served in the United States Army as a 54B, Nuclear Biological Chemical Specialist for 89th Chemical Company, 3rd Armored Calvary Regiment. Marcia currently manages national property tax compliance for Comcast and is also the leader of the Comcast Veterans Network.

WHAT IS COMCAST CORPORATION?

Comcast Corporation is the nation's leading provider of entertainment, information, and communication products and services. The company develops, manages, and operates cable systems in 39 states and the District of Columbia. Comcast Corporation also owns a 51% controlling interest in NBCUniversal, with GE holding a 49% stake.

WHAT IS THE COMCAST VETERANS NETWORK?

Comcast Veterans Network (VetNet) Affinity Group was launched in Philadelphia in January 2012 and currently has 80 members. Future chapters in other cities will be launched in the near future. Our mission is to support and develop our Comcast veterans, reservists, and active military employees through professional development and networking and to engage our local communities by raising awareness and support for the needs of our veterans and their families.

WHAT DOES THE COMCAST VETERANS NETWORK DO FOR VETS?

Comcast is proud to join other leading companies in corporate America in attracting, employing, and supporting our active duty military service members, reservists, and veterans. A responsible corporate citizen, Comcast is a leader in supporting our heroes through programs such as our annual Holiday Troop Greetings and the "Hire A VeteranOnDemand" initiative, which connects job-seeking veterans with local employers. We are committed to opening avenues to our outstanding career opportunities through targeted outreach to the military and veteran community, while military friendly policies and benefits are in place to support those of us who continue to serve as part of the National Guard or Reserves. Comcast veterans are invited to join our VetNet Affinity Group and are well represented on our new corporate Joint Diversity Council. Like those who have served in the military, Comcast shares the values of leadership, service, teamwork, and ethics, and we are proud partners with those who currently serve our nation and a supportive employer of the veterans and reservists who have joined our ranks.

HOW CAN VETS LEARN MORE ABOUT THE COMCAST VETERANS NETWORK?

Veterans can find out about career opportunities and contact the company through the web at http://www.comcast-jobs.com/.

11 GENERAL ORDERS OF NETWORKING

1. To smile and deliver a firm handshake when meeting someone.
2. To do my research and know something about the person or people I'm meeting.
3. To give my undivided attention and to look the other person in the eye when engaged in a conversation.
4. To actively listen to what the other person is saying instead of waiting for my turn to talk.
5. To call the person by their name when greeting them or saying good-bye.
6. To wear a lapel pin that represents my military unit or branch of service.
7. To follow up with all new contacts or meetings within 24 hours.
8. To be a resource for others by giving generously of my time and expertise.
9. To always have a business card available.
10. To have a list of "get to know you" questions always at the ready.
11. To take the initiative and approach others with positive expectations and genuine interest.

EVENT CHECKLIST

The following checklist will help you get the most out of any business event where you are expected to meet and connect with prospects and other people to add to your networking universe. Your objective is to reach out, take the initiative, make a positive impression, and your ability to capitalize on contacts and connections will be a key part of your continued career success.

BEFORE YOU GO

- ☐ Do your research. Find out all you can about the event, including any interesting and important facts about the location, its purpose, the organization sponsoring it, and people likely to attend. Think about your reason for attending this event—is it a group you wish to join, are you already involved, what is the specific goal for this meeting? Check the website to find out who the organizer is, who is on the advisory board, and what the mission and agenda is.
- ☐ Identify who you'd like to meet. Think strategically about those attending. Set a goal to research three to five people you would like to meet. Also consider calling or emailing ahead of time to introduce yourself to those hosting or planning the event—you will stand out.
- ☐ Prepare your "intangible tool kit," your "state of mind" to engage fully and productively.
- ☐ Have a positive attitude. Be ready to engage and enjoy the prospect of meeting new people and reconnecting with those you know.
- ☐ Have self-confidence. Remember what you have to offer as a military veteran and be proud of your service.
  - – Have a 20- to 30-second introduction prepared for this event. Think about how you wish to be remembered; What is your "headline" and benefit statement, and why should they care.
- ☐ Have an open mind. Go without any immediate expectations—except to learn, connect, and give away something. Believe that there is someone there who you can learn from and give something away to (a piece of advice or information).
- ☐ Be present. Respect yourself and others—turn off or put all electronic devices on silent to avoid distractions.

☐ Actively listen. Talk less and listen more—(monitor yourself not to interrupt and to show you are also listening; remember the color of the eyes of the person you are talking with). Remember names by forming an impression; repeat their name back and form a quick association.

☐ Smile. Have a ready and genuine smile to show your interest and approachability (also a great confidence booster!).

☐ Have a firm handshake. Make a positive connection.

 – Ears and eyes—open and ready to connect

 – Your presence—dress for the event. What is your signature "prop"? Appearance speaks volumes.

☐ Prepare your "tangible tool kit." Keep these handy to help you meet and follow up with ease.

 ☐ Breath mints—simple and often overlooked.

 ☐ Hand sanitizer—no need to be compulsive, however you will be shaking a lot of hands.

 ☐ Business cards—an adequate supply, in good condition; always have them with you.

 ☐ Card case—take one for your cards and one for those you collect (keep in separate pockets).

 ☐ A nice pen—an accessory for your image (in fact, carry two in case the ink runs out).

 ☐ A small notepad—to jot down things you learn immediately after speaking with someone who you will follow up with (for example, their preferred method of communication, what you promised in your follow-up, what you remember about them).

 ☐ Notecards and stamps—be prepared with the notecards stamped and you can easily follow up immediately with a quick thank-you note to those you connected with. You will stand out with this 45-cent investment plan.

 ☐ Highlighter—highlight your name tag. It's a conversation starter.

 ☐ Name tag—place it on your right side, to be seen as people shake your right hand (the way our eyes naturally look).

 ☐ Mirror—do a quick pre-check to make sure you look neat, tidy, and have a genuine smile, and give yourself a quick mental pep talk ("I'm happy to be here, I've set a goal, I'm excited to learn and connect").

☐ Prepare your "opening line." Think in advance of what you will say as you meet people for the first time

 – Think of "open-ended" questions to start a conversation.

  • "What brought you to the meeting?"

- • "I'm thinking of joining this group. Are you a member? Tell me a bit about what you like."
- • "Hello, I don't believe we have met yet, I'm _____ and you are?"

☐ Have a list of "get to know you" questions. Prepare some questions that help you build rapport as you are connecting and keep the conversation going. From your research in advance about the group and association, you will already have some material to frame your questions.
  – "What are some trends going on in your business/field?"
  – "How would I know if I'm speaking to someone you would like to meet or could possibly use your services or that of your firm?"
  – "What do you do when you are not working?"

☐ Develop a list of "idea generator" topics (small talk). Become conversant about current affairs, best-selling books, movies, business news, the stock market, and certainly the latest news and trends in the financial industry and your special niche. Keep a running journal of such topic ideas organized by subject so you are always prepared. Every day, read your preferred news medium for general news, industry news, and firm news so that you have topics ready to discuss.

☐ Prepare a 30-second introduction about yourself. Be ready to easily and confidently answer the inevitable question of "What do you do?" Plan positive and interesting "sound bites" and a provocative value proposition about you and your company that will get people interested enough in you to get to know you better. Rehearse in front of a mirror or tape yourself until you're fluent and sound comfortable. Keep practicing. This will vary according to the event, audience, and person you are talking with, but the core message will be consistent. Practice how you can change accordingly. The true goal is to say enough to get interest and then move the conversation to what the other person does. That will help you reframe how you will continue saying what you do.

  Reminders as you prepare:
  – Who are you?
  – Who do you work with (target market)?
  – What solutions do you provide?
  – What is the benefit you offer?
  – What differentiates you?

☐ Set a goal for the event. Make it specific and strategic for your business situation and needs. Be realistic and know that for your goal to be a reality you have to follow up and take the action steps after the event.

☐ Be ready to take the initiative. Whether you are an extrovert or introvert, plan to approach others with positive expectations and genuine interest. Besides the people you identified in advance who you hope to possibly meet—remember to say hello to these folks and to maximize your attendance:

– Greeter and/or organizer
– People you meet in line as you are checking in
– Those in line to get a drink or food
– Someone standing alone

Remember, you only have to say hello, smile, and be pleasant. You will not have a full conversation with everyone you meet, yet you never know unless you reach out.

DURING THE EVENT

☐ Take a deep breath. You have arrived, you've done your homework, and you're ready!

☐ Introduce yourself to the host. Seek them out and make a personal connection. Again—you will stand out.

☐ Get in line. An easy and effortless way to engage people, whether it's at the registration desk, the coat check, or in front of the food and beverage area.

☐ Dive in! Look for a group of people who are smiling and engaged; say hello and engage them. Walk up to a group of at least three people—when it is just two people, they are already deep in conversation.

☐ Start a conversation with your dinner partner. If there is a meal involved, talk to those on either side of you, and even across the table when it is feasible. Make a point to sit with new people.

☐ Make connections and a plan to follow up. Have a goal to learn something about each person you meet and create reasons to follow up and start building a rapport and hopefully a relationship.

☐ Listen and learn. Ask about the other person first. Remember that true networking is about giving without concern that you will get something back. Make a point to actively listen and you will learn something new and useful. Listen with your eyes and ears, don't interrupt, and jot down later what you learned. (I am amazed about the information I pick up when I least expect it.) Be sure to ask them what they do—people love to talk about themselves and their interests and you will be remembered as a good conversationalist because you listened.

☐ Find preferred methods of communication. Every busy person has a preferred method of communication. Ask, "what is your preferred method of communication for us to connect?" (email, telephone, text)

Remember one size does not fit all—make it easy for the person to reply to you when you reach out. Ask them in advance.

☐ Have an exit strategy. At events, everyone wants to talk and mingle. If you have made a concrete connection, you will have your agenda to follow up—when and how. To diplomatically disengage at the event—depending again on if you are going to follow up or it was someone you only talked with briefly at the event:

– "It was great to meet you and I look forward to continuing our conversation. As you mentioned, I will follow up with you _____ (when they told you to follow up) and via _____ (their communication preference)."

– "It was great chatting with you—enjoy the rest of your time here."

– "I'm very glad we met. I wish you continued success and if I have an opportunity or suggestion for you, I will definitely be in touch."

– "My time has already been well spent—I'm glad we had a chance to meet."

– "I look forward to seeing you at another event. Thank you and enjoy the rest of the meeting."

AFTER THE EVENT

☐ Within 24 hours, send an email, and for those with whom you really wish to start the connection, write a handwritten note, simple and sincere, stating your pleasure in meeting them, your appreciation of their time, and any information you promised to send.

☐ If you promised to send materials, do so immediately. Many people say they will do something after an event; those who actually follow up promptly will always stand out. Send only what you promised—less is more—you will have time to bring more as you deepen the connection.

☐ Call or email within two weeks after the event to suggest a meeting with those that said they would enjoy the next step. Be strategic in your follow-up. If there was interest in further contact after the event, be the one to follow up with something specific, suggesting an activity, time, and place.

☐ If a contact of yours provided you with a referral, be ready to tell them of follow-up results. Polite and smart business practice is to let people know what happened, to keep them in the loop about next steps and, of course, to give a sincere thank you for the connection and introduction.

Remember the "event" is only the starting point. To build strong connections into your universal network, you must take the next steps to build the relationship and do so consistently.

Have a 24/7 networking awareness: We can meet and connect with people any time and anywhere.

1. Jay Yarow and Kamelia Angeloval, "Internet Advertising Ready to Take More Money Away from Newspapers," January 5, 2010, http://articles.businessinsider.com/2010-01-05/tech/30051606_1_advertisers-newspapers-web.

2. "The Rapid Decline in Conference Attendance: Why It's Happening and How a High Quality Agenda Can Help," *Tradeshow Magazine,* http://www.trade-show-expo.com/2010_TSE_pages/050110_CEIR_index.html

3. http://www.newspaperdeathwatch.com, accessed Tuesday, September 25, 2010.

4. Even Wall Street acknowledges that the days of printed directories like the yellow pages are numbered. The *Wall Street Journal* reported that advertising in U.S. print directories is expected to fall 39% over the next four years. In their words *"as people migrate enmasse to the web."*

5. Bruce Barton, "Television Advertising: An Irreversible Decline?" *Contacto Magazine*. http://www.contactomagazine.com/biznews/tvadvertisingslump0309.html

6. Robert Putnam, *Bowling Alone,* Simon & Schuster, NY, August 2001.

7. Pew Project for the Excellence in Journalism. http://www.journalism.org

8. Joseph Sexmith and Robert Angel, "Social Networking: The View from the C-Suite," Ivey Business Journal, July/August 2009.

9. Erik Qualman, *Socialnomics: How Social Media Transforms the Way We Live and Do Business.* Wiley, 2009.

10. Ibid.

11. Ibid.

12. William Jackson, "African Americans; Techology and Social Media," The Florida Times-Union, December 27, 2011, http://jacksonville.com/opinion/blog/william-jacksons-blog

13. American Marketing Association, Jupiter Survey, 2009, http://www.marketingpower.com/ResourceLibrary/Documents/AMA_Surveys/2009_AMA_Social_Media_Survey.pdf. Accessed March 12, 2012.

14. Mary Madden, "State of Social Media: 2011," December 14, 2011, http://pewinternet.org/Presentations/2011/Dec/State-of-Social-Media.aspx.

15. Noah Elkin, "How America Searches: Health and Wellness," January 14, 2008, http://www.icrossing.com/sites/default/files/how-america-searches-health-and-wellness.pdf.

16. "IDC State of Social Business," January 2010, IDC Corporate, USA, http://idc.com.

17. "Mobile Social Networking Use Grows 182% over 2007 in U.S.," The Kelsey Group and ConStat, December 2008.

18. Mary Madden and Kathryn Zickuhr, "65% of Online Adults Use Social Networking," August 26, 2011, The Pew Research Center, http://www.pewinternet.org/Reports/2011/Social-Networking-Sites/Overview.aspx

OTHER RESOURCES

Michael Faulkner. Author polls initiated on LinkedIn, 2009. http://polls.linkedin.com/.

Forrester NACTAS, Q2. 2006. Youth, Media, and Marketing and Financial Online Survey. Cambridge, MA, http://www.forrester.com/consumer?N=10004+5018#/meet+your+next+financial+consumer/quickscan/-/E-RES41529, accessed September 3, 2012.

Clifford F. Gray and Erik W. Larson. Project Management: The Managerial Process. 4th ed. New York: McGraw-Hill/Irwin, 2007.

Peter D. Hart Research Associates: "How Should Colleges Prepare Students to Succeed in Today's Global Economy?" December 28, 2006, www.aacu.org/leap/documents/Re8097abcombined.pdf.

Andrea Nierenberg. *Nonstop Networking*. Sterling, VA: Capital Books. 2002.

"Strengths-Based Devlopment: Using Strengths to Accelerate Performance," from Gallup Poll Social Series: Values and Beliefs, field date: 5/7/2009–5/10/2009, www.gallup.com/consulting/61/Strengths-Development.aspx.

Mail Preference Service, Direct Marketing Association, PO Box 9008, Farmingdale, NY 11735-9008.